C.A.R.E.

C.A.R.E.

Created for Wholeness

Patricia Warford, PsyD

WIPF & STOCK · Eugene, Oregon

C.A.R.E.
Created for Wholeness

Wipf & Stock
An Imprint of Wipf and Stock Publishers
199 W. 8th Ave., Suite 3
Eugene, OR 97401

www.wipfandstock.com

ISBN 13: 978-1-62564-124-3

Manufactured in the U.S.A.

For Candice

Contents

Introduction

THIS BOOK STARTED WITH an evening presentation at a women's retreat entitled "Embracing Life." It was then expanded into a monthly series called "Straight Talk." The guiding principle was to understand God's design for healthy development using Erik Erikson's Stages of Psychosocial Development as a template. Erikson's stages delineate healthy developmental progression throughout the life span. Additionally, Erikson understood that environment may prevent healthy progression and he identified the consequences for failing to successfully complete the stage.

Those familiar with Erikson's work will note I have rearranged identity, intimacy, and generativity into intimacy, generativity, and identity. Erikson believed females followed his stages from trust through industry. After the industry stage, he believed, women went into a state of psychosocial moratorium where they remained until they found a man to bring into their inner circle and were complete. He wrote this in 1968, the beginning of the second wave of the Women's Movement. Needless to say, female writers bashed his ideas. Because they were female writers, they were labeled feminists. To Erickson's credit, he wrote a follow-up piece in 1972 in which he acknowledged that his female critics were correct. He instructed the boys in the ivory towers to allow women to define women's stages.

Nancy Chodorow took up Erickson's call for women to define women's developmental stages. Chodorow proposed that women's stages followed a pattern of continued connection. Subsequent research supported her position. Instead of following Erickson stages (identity, intimacy, and generativity), we will follow female stages of development: intimacy, generativity, and identity. Although almost twenty years have passed since I looked at the literature, some believe Erikson's stages, with their emphasis on autonomy and separation, follow a dominant culture (white, middle-class, male) while these alternate stages, with their emphasis on connectedness and relationship, follow a non-dominant culture (women, the poor, minorities.) As such, I wonder if this progression would better fit Christians.

Failure to successfully attain the goal of a stage has historically placed responsibility on the individual, without due diligence to trauma and abuse as sources of impediment. The role of abuse in the failure to successfully progress became clearer for me in preparing for the "Straight Talk" series. Abuse disrupts healthy development. Sadly, the home is the most likely place for a child to experience abuse and trauma. The most likely perpetrator of abuse is someone known to the child. For women age fourteen and older, the most likely perpetrator of abuse against her is her intimate male partner.

As harm is done in the context of relationship, healing can only be done in the context of relationship. The triune God has existed in relationship throughout eternity. This relational God created, reconciled, and empowered humanity. Sin and the fall introduced abuse, as well as disconnection from God, ourselves, and others. The interplay between these two became the title of the book and the outline of each chapter. C.A.R.E. stands for Created by God, Abused by people, Reconciled to Christ, and Empowered by the Holy Spirit.

The concept of created by God, reconciled to Christ, and empowered by the Holy Spirit are separated here for the purposes of progression. But this is a false division. Christianity has historically espoused belief in a triune God—the mystery of the one God in three Persons. The Trinity is one. Christianity is monotheistic. In and through YHWH we are created, reconciled, and empowered. We were created by God, were reconciled to God through his work on the cross, and are empowered by God for the potential of reconciliation to others who choose reconciliation.

Scripture portrays men as both godly and ungodly and women as both godly and ungodly. Too often Christian women have limited archetypes for being female. The dominant archetype has been the Madonna (meaning Mary, the mother of Jesus, not the modern singer) or the whore (as Mary Magdalene is often misrepresented.) Women cannot attain the perfection of the first and fear the label of the second. Most women are familiar with ungodly women, usually women who have "seduced" men: Jezebel, Gomer, Delilah, Bathsheba. Godly women, or women viewed as heroines, will dominate in this work. Also, women in Scripture represent a great diversity of experience. The Bible does not shy away from our worth nor our suffering. Women of the Bible are not two-dimensional characters with cliché answers. They are flesh-and-blood beings who love and feel and struggle. The women presented here will either depict the healthy or unhealthy aspect of the stage. Sometimes unhealthy development is due to abuse; sometimes the environment attempts to place the unhealthy aspect upon her. Because one way of objectifying a person is to refer to her by her label ("woman at the well"), I will give her a name. Where I have been able to find a name in the historical record, I will use that. Where I have not been able to find a name, I will give her one. God knows her name.

Healthy development is interrupted by abuse. Abuse is defined as:

> A pattern of *coercive behavior* used by one person to *control and subordinate* another in an *intimate relationship*. These behaviors include physical, sexual, psychological, and economic abuse. Tactics of coercion, terrorism, degradation, exploitation, and violence are used to *engender fear* in the victim in order to *enforce compliance*.[1]

Healthy development is premised on support in self-determination, which grows into love, authentic mutuality, and relationship. Abuse by definition is about domination, fear, and forced compliance. Again, the home is the most likely place women and children experience abuse. (Adult males are most likely to be victims of male stranger violence.)

Another premise I hold is a distinction between self-worth, self-esteem, and self-image.[2] Self-esteem is based on what you do. Healthy self-esteem recognizes that you do some things well and some things not so well. Balancing what you do well and what you do poorly provides grounding. The word "and" here is important. The word "but" negates whatever goes before it. The word "and" holds both the predecessor and successor to be true. If you only present what you do well, that is grandiosity. If you only present what you do poorly, that is shame. Healthy self-esteem allows a healthy pride in your God-given talents and gifts while acknowledging your limitations as a human.

Self-image is what is reflected back to us by others. When we hold an infant and smile into her eyes, we are communicating, "You are wonderful!" When we are talking to people and they are maintaining eye

---

1. See http://www.cadreprogram.org/downloads_files/cadre%20dv.pdf, p. 2; italics added.

2. Dr. Scott Willis presented this in a lecture for the graduate course Existential Psychotherapy at George Fox University. Used with permission.

contact and expressing in their body language that they are listening and connecting with us, our self-image is enhanced. When we are talking to someone and they are yawning, looking away, or looking bored, our self-image takes a hit.

So, stop for a minute and consider this question before reading on: If self-esteem is based on what you do and self-image is based on what is reflected back to you from others, what is self-worth based on? Thought about it? Most people tend to say, "How I see myself." Actually, how we see ourselves is often more based on self-image and on how others see us, especially how our primary caretakers communicated how they saw us. Self-worth is based solely on the fact that you were created in the image of God. If I look at you in a way that enhances your self-image, I am merely acknowledging the image of God that YHWH placed in you. If I look at you in a way that harms your self-image, I am coming from my own sinful nature. Your worth is not mine (or anybody else's) to give; I am not God. Nor is your worth mine (or anybody else's) to take away. As we will see, God literally put the image of God in you.

1

Before You Were Born

Oh yes, you shaped me first inside, then out;
you formed me in my mother's womb.
I thank you, High God—you're breathtaking!
Body and soul, I am marvelously made!
I worship in adoration—what a creation!
You know me inside and out,
you know every bone in my body;
You know exactly how I was made, bit by bit,
how I was sculpted from nothing into something.
Like an open book, you watched me grow
from conception to birth;
all the stages of my life were spread out before you.

PSALM 139:13–18 (*THE MESSAGE*)

Created by God

THE FIRST THING THAT God decided was your sex. Sex is biologically determined; gender is a social construct which changes according to particular societal norms. God determined your sex. YHWH took the X chromosome from your mother and the X chromosome from your father. Your sex was determined: you are female. Then YHWH sealed them together with laminin. Laminin is a molecule which plays a major role in your going from nothing to something. Laminin plays a role in telling cells where to go in the body, what to become, and how to hold together. Simply put, laminin sends cells to the bottom of your feet and the top of your head. It decides which cell will become an eyeball and which will become a toenail. It will glue the cells together into a cohesive whole. Laminin will be found in every muscle and organ. It will be in skin, the body's largest organ.

Laminin

The most interesting thing about laminin is its molecular structure: the molecular structure of laminin is in the shape of a cross. This was the first act of trust in your existence. God entrusted you with the image of Christ. The days, weeks, and months that followed sculpted you bit by bit so that by birth everything you needed to survive is there and you were designed for relationship.

Although two X chromosomes (as compared to an X and a Y chromosome, for males) determines your sex, it will be months before organs differentiating sex are present. Initially the fetus appears genderless. The bonding of the two X chromosomes provides genetic codes or DNA. As the cells divide, the brain, spine, heart, and digestive system begin to form. Eyes, nose, and ears begin to take shape. Awareness of surroundings begins. Hearing and the ability to speak language, any and every language, is present. Communication of needs is available. All of this is designed to relate and learn and grow through relationship and communication with another. By birth, the largest organ, skin, requires the life-giving power of touch. DNA will determine everything physically about you: the color of your hair, eyes, and skin. It will provide guidelines for height and shape of you and your parts. And it will take a lot of energy to keep all this going. That's where mitochondrial DNA or mtDNA comes in.

DNA and mtDNA

mtDNA is a structure within cells that converts food into energy (or power) in a form the cell can use. While DNA comes from both our male and female ancestors, mtDNA is passed solely from our female ancestors. This is true for both men and women. Many women believe that God created women as an afterthought. But God's design is to have us there from the beginning. Through mtDNA, we are all linked to the first mother, Eve.

Eve

Adam and Eve were created for relationship. God created them for relationship first with YHWH, then with each other. In the beginning, God created the human. *Adam* literally means "human" or, as in some translations, "the man." Adam was molded from earth (neutral in English), or *adamah* (feminine in the original Hebrew). So Adam (masculine) came from adamah. "The Adam" or "the human" was gender neutral. Both male and female were present in the human (Gen 1:28; 5:2). The Adam is the only one, unlike the animals who had companions (i.e., the lion and the lioness, the bull and the cow). YHWH stated that it was "not good" for the Adam to be alone, or the only one of its kind, and put the human in a deep sleep. Separating the human, "the Adam" became gendered. Adamah brought forth the Adam and from Adam came Eve. Eve became the companion.

Helpmate, or *ezer*, is used twenty times in the Old Testament: three times for military ally or aide and seventeen times for God. The Psalmist said, "I lift up my eyes . . . where does my help come from? My help comes from the Lord" (Ps 121:1–3). The Lord is my helper. YHWH is my ezer. It is also used for Eve. Ezer is not weak. Ezer is one who has the power and strength to help. Ezer has the mtDNA.

In Genesis, the one who names has dominion over the one named. "The Adam" named the animals that were brought to see if a companion could be found. Unlike the animals, when Adam calls Eve "woman," he is calling her what God had already named (Gen 2:22–23). Like "the human," her name "woman" was God given. She was present when God instructed *them* to have dominion (Gen 1:28).

God set out the form relationships would take in the perfect world God created. First, God modeled the role of the spoken word as a means to bring forth life. "God said," and life came into being. The man and the woman would rule over the animals God had created (Gen 1:26). Together they would be fruitful and subdue the earth (Gen 1:28). God sets the man and woman in the garden to tend it. Eve was to be Adam's dearest friend and companion. Together they faced the world and their future.

Abused by People

The Fall

Then came the fall. And the curse. Genesis 3:16–19 has been viewed as either descriptive or prescriptive. Descriptive interpretation construes the curse as God describing to Adam and Eve the impact of sin on gender roles. Prescriptive interpretation construes the curse as God mandating future gender roles. I hold the former view. Because sin now entered the world, the egalitarian relationship designed by God was lost to the sinful desire to dominate another human.

Many argue that Eve was responsible for the fall, using 2 Timothy. The passage in Timothy is difficult and won't be tackled here. Suffice it to say that while Paul appears to hold Eve responsible in 2 Timothy, Paul holds Adam responsible as the cause of death for all in 1 Corinthians (15:22). Paul uses metaphorical language distinguishing the first Adam (of Genesis) from the second Adam (Jesus Christ). The Old Testament holds the Hebrews responsible for their own behaviors whether in the wilderness or as the cause of the devastation of the kingdom. Both Adam and Eve sinned. Both brought sin and its consequences into the world. Both need a redeemer.

Abuse Violates God's Mandate in the Garden of Eden

In Genesis 1:26–28 (CEB),

> God said, "Let us make humanity in our image to resemble us so that they may take charge of the fish of the sea, the birds in the sky, the livestock, all the earth, and all the crawling things on earth." God created humanity in God's own image, in the divine image God created them, male and female God created them. God blessed them and said to them, "Be fertile and multiply; fill the earth and master it. Take charge of the fish of the sea, the birds in the sky, and everything crawling on the ground."

"Them" and "they" refer to the "male and female." God said "they may take charge of." And "God created humanity in God's own image, in the divine image God created them, male and female God created them" (1:27). Spiritual abuse denies the person the God-given worth as one created in the image of God. Examples of spiritual abuse include misusing Scripture to force compliance. This is often done in the claim of making a woman "submissive." To force submission is called oppression, and Scripture distinctly stands against oppression. Submission can only be freely given. Another example of spiritual abuse is to claim "headship" that does not follow Jesus' example and explicit statement that a leader is one who is the servant (Matt 20:26; Mark 10:43). Headship or leadership that demands submission is spiritual abuse. Headship or leadership which inspires submission is following Christ. Using Scriptures that supports a self-serving position or merely for the sake of argument is abusive and violates the Spirit of Peace.

Physical violence is the most commonly perceived type of abuse. While physical abuse includes hitting or punching, it also includes pushing, shoving, body checking (bumping with chest or shoulder), kicking, hitting with objects (objects may be thrown or swung), spitting, kneeing, grabbing, or elbowing. Choking is something one does when an object such as food stuck in the throat; when someone blocks another's airway either by putting hand(s) around throat or over nose or mouth, it is call strangulation. Physical violence is *not* the *only* type of abuse.

Verbal abuse is a much more common form of abuse. Verbal abuse violates the model YHWH gave in "God said," bringing forth creation and life. The childhood verse "sticks and stones make break my bones" is more accurately completed with the phrase "but words will wound my soul!" Verbal abuse includes name-calling, as well as threats, mocking, sarcasm, and swearing. Verbal abuse does not have to include yelling. One can be verbally abusive in a calm, soft tone.

Sexual abuse includes rape but is not limited to rape. Sexual abuse includes speech which is disrespectful in a sexual way. It includes pressure or coercion for sex, withholding sex, affairs, engaging in porn or with those who are sex trafficked, pouting when not given sex, exposing someone to sex that is inappropriate for their age, self gratifying in a sexual way that is unwanted by the other party. Whether the "f-bomb" constitutes sexual abuse frequently becomes a discussion in our groups—the groups always decide that it does.

The most common form of abuse is neglect. Cain asks God, "Am I my brother's keeper?" God answers by giving the law that includes rules for the just treatment of others. Jesus states that the two great commandments are: love God and love your neighbor. James 4:17 says, "To him that knows to do good and does it not, it is sin." Neglect includes ignoring the needs of those God has given you to care for. Placing your wants (such as feeding an addiction) before providing for the needs of your family can be a form of neglect. We truly can live without having what we want; our basic needs are necessary to sustain life. Basic needs include food, clothing, and emotional needs. Some dictionaries include "disregard" in their definitions for neglect, and disregard is defined as "to treat somebody or something with disrespect."

Abuse is a means to an end. Abuse is a behavior intended to gain power and control over another human being that wounds the body, soul, or spirit. It takes many forms. It damages and destroys our bodies and our souls. It negatively impacts our relationship to ourselves, to others, and to God. The following lists provide examples of abuse:

Types of Psychological and Spiritual Abuse

Acting superior, boss, or king

Any abuse listed

Being possessive or jealous

Censoring mail or telephone use

Checking up

Comparing

Controlling car keys or use

Controlling cash, checkbook, money, or information

Controlling social or family contacts

Crazy-making

Criticizing children, parenting, family, or homemaking

Demanding acceptance of own point of view

Double messages

Driving recklessly

Exhibiting strength, size

Expecting accounting for activities

Expecting check-ins

Following

Forced to apologize

Forced to submit

Glaring

Going out and leaving partner without information

Forcing religious beliefs or attendance

Harass hang-up phone calls

Ignoring

Ignoring children

Isolating

Insulting appearance

Interrupting sleep or eating

Lying

Mind games

Not allowing church, school, work

Preventing use of phone

Stalking

Standing over

Staring

Tellling secrets

Threatening to harm or kill

Threatening with a weapon

Using Bible or God to justify abuse

Using religion to justify abuse

Using religious superiority

Types of Physical Abuse

Backhanding

Bearhugging

Beating

Bending fingers or arms

Biting

Blocking an airway (mouth, nose, throat)

Blocking movements

Body-checking

Breaking bones

Burning or electrocuting

Carrying against will

Destroying personal items

Elbowing

Grabbing

Hand over mouth, nose, throat

Headlocking

Holding

Hurting when pregnant

Injuring with weapon or vehicle

Kicking

Kneeing

Picking up

Pinching

Pointing

Poking (eyes, arm, chest, etc.)

Pulling hair

Punching

Pushing or shoving

Restraining

Scratching

Sitting or laying on

Slapping

Smothering

Spanking

Spitting on

Squeezing

Standing over

Stepping on

Stepping on feet

Suffocating

Tearing clothes

Throwing bodily

Throwing food, drink, objects

Tying up or locking in room

Urinating or defecating on

Wrestling

Types of Property Abuse

Breaking objects

Driving wrecklessly

Pulling phone from wall

Punching walls

Slamming doors

Throwing objects

Types of Sexual Abuse

Accusations of affairs

Affairs or threats of affairs

Bestiality

Bondage or Sado-masochism

Coercing sexual contactCoercing unwanted types of sexual contact

Comparing sexual performance to others

Demanding certain clothing or undergarments

Demanding sex

Demanding unwanted types of sex

Expecting sex during pregnancy

Expecting sex after childbirth

Expecting sex after surgery

Expecting sexual duties

Exposing

Forced Exhibitionism

Forcing sexual activities

Grabbing sexually

Including other unwanted partners

Insulting or degrading body image

Insulting performance

Negative comments about menstruation

Negative comments about PMS

Not cooperating in birth control

Pornography

Public fondling or comments

Rape

Sexual names

- -Cunt
- -Prick
- -Slut
- -Split tail
- -Tramp
- -Twat
- -Whore

Sexual terms (ex, "fucking stupid")

Sexual jokes

Transmitting diseases

Unwanted bruises

Unwanted hickeys

Unwanted ripping clothes off

Unwanted rough sex

Unwanted use of objects

Using prostitution/prostituting her

Verbal pushing into sex

Voyeurism

Withholding sex

Types of Child Abuse

Alienating child

Any other abuse listed

Bribing child

Child witnessing violence

Identity theft from child

Types of Verbal Abuse

Accusations	-Lazy
Cursing	-Stupid
Getting the last word	-Ugly
Harassment	Refusing to talk
Insulting	Screaming
Name Calling:	Talking over
-Bitch	Threats
-Fat	Yelling

Types of Animal Abuse

Abandoning animal	Neglecting animal
Beating animal	Poaching
Kicking animal	Shooting at animal
Killing animal	Throwing animals
-except hunting/mercy	

Reconciled to Christ

Restore, Redeem, and Reconcile

God did not leave us without hope. Three terms are closely related: restore, redeem, and reconcile. Restore is to return someone to a previously held rank, office, or position. Redeem is to recover ownership by paying a specified sum. Reconcile is to make one thing compatible with another, bring into harmony.

Throughout Scripture God restores things. Jesus and Joseph are the only individuals restored to positions. Both had been unjustly accused and imprisoned. God does not restore a person to a position of power where they had been abusive; sometimes YHWH delays and takes positions away from the offspring rather than the person. Neither does God ever restore an abused person to an abusive situation. The prophets warn that God harshly judges oppression (Isa 1:17; Jer 50:33; Ezek 22:7; Dan 4:27; Zeph 3:19; Zech 11:11).

Two redeemers in Scripture are Jesus and Boaz. Boaz "buys" the land owned by his deceased relatives and "acquires" Ruth (Ruth 4:5, 7). He does not buy Ruth, he redeems her. Jesus pays a price needed for our redemption but calls us to be friends (John 15:15).

Reconciliation is not the same as restoration. Restoration is to return to one's former state. Abuse undermines compatibility and harmony. Reconciliation brings two into harmony. If the former state of the relationship was abusive, the new state of the relationship, by definition, has to be different. Reconciliation can only happen when both parties admit the relationship was disrupted, require accountability within the relationship, and move toward harmony.

Harmony

The road to harmony will have periods of disharmony. Think of it as an orchestra. Beginning band students need practice to make their own instruments do anything more than screech. Over time, the students make their instruments sing but may still not be in harmony with other instruments. Timid band members may need to play louder. Loud band members may need to learn to listen to their band mates. They play simple pieces together. They learn to synchronize timing. Eventually, the band improves enough to play harder pieces. They move from band to orchestra.

Many people see reconciliation as a point in time rather than a journey. They don't take the time needed for this journey. Sometimes they just don't have the capability. Sometimes they fear letting others in. Sometimes they want to avoid disharmony, even if it is temporary. Or any number of other reasons. Tragically, they never get beyond the beginner band class. They can play simple pieces. And play them well. But "Twinkle, Twinkle, Little Star" will never have the majesty of a Handel's *Messiah* or the *William Tell Overture*. God calls us to play in the orchestra. YHWH smiles at the student playing in the high school gym, but God *beams* when that student matures and develops the skill needed to play Carnegie Hall. We choose whether our reconciliation will stay in the high school gym or we will play at Carnegie Hall.

Things we see exist in space; things we hear exist in time. Harmony exists in time. While it is not tangible, it is real. Harmony does not exist in a point in time; it is a flow between two or more musicians. Paul understood this. In 2 Corinthians 5:17–20, Paul writes that God reconciled us to God through Christ and has given us the ministry and message of reconciliation. The movement of this passage is musical! Reconciliation is not a point in time. It began at a point in time: at the cross. It continues in the work of the Holy Spirit, who desires to move us from novice band student to skilled musician. God began this work of reconciliation before you were born (1 Pet 1:18–20).

Empowered by the Holy Spirit

Life-Giving Breath

YHWH formed "the adam" from "the adamah." *Adamah* is the Hebrew word for earth. Adamah is a feminine. At the beginning of the Bible are these three: YHWH (Triune God), adamah (feminine), and adam (masculine). God bent down and breathed into the adam and the adam became a living being. God breathed (ruah) into the human. The word implies breath, it also implies spirit. In the beginning of humanity, God empowered the mound of clay to become a living being by inbreathing the Spirit.

The Spirit empowered the individual with life-giving breath; the Spirit also empowered the church. While the Spirit is seen in the Old Testament as "falling" on the prophets (1 Sam 11:6), the Spirit comes on women in the New Testament. Mary, "filled with the Spirit," proclaims the glory of God. On the birthday of the church, the day of Pentecost, the Spirit filled the men and women who were in the upper room. The Spirit empowered them to boldly live the gospel. In fact, the church itself is referred to in the feminine: the Bride of Christ.

To Be Known

This chapter began with Psalm 139. Throughout the psalm, the writer expresses amazement at the depth and breadth of God's knowledge of the writer. From nothing to something and from conception to birth God is hands-on. The word "formed" is "wove" in a different translation. The metaphor of a weaver is used for God. Die-hard weavers make their own yarn. They choose the source: goat, sheep, llama. From the source, they prepare the wool. They comb it, spin it, and dye it. They envision their creation before they begin. They touch every skein. They run their hand over the work as it is taking shape. When they put on the final touches, they stand back and admire their work. They repeat the words of God at creation: It is good.

C.A.R.E.

All of this is past. Then one of the most miraculous, marvelous moments in all of creation happened: you were born. The birth was messy. It was painful. It was *beautiful*.

2

Trust

Yet you brought me out of the womb;
you made me trust in you, even at my mother's breast.

PSALM 22:9

Created by God

To Explore a Trustworthy World

The first of Erikson's stages is trust. When you were first born, gender was a non-concept to you. God created you with the ability to get your needs met. And you had a drive to get your needs met and to live. You cried and something in the universe took care of it. You trusted this "something" to meet your needs. Trust is defined as the "reliance on the integrity, strength, ability, surety of a person or thing." You cried and you were fed, changed, or rocked. Over time, you came to realize that this "something" was another being. First God trusts you by putting the image of YWHW in you both figuratively and literally (laminin). Then you trusted your universe. God created you to trust, to be loved and to be known.

From the very beginning of your life, you interacted with your world. Your smile warmed the hearts of those who saw it and responded by holding you and smiling back. Every time you did something for the first time was a milestone and cause for celebration. The first time you latched on to suck was a drive for life. The first wet diaper, even the first dirty diaper, elicited excitement. Sitting up. Reaching out. Crawling. Standing. First sounds, then intonation, eventually recognizable sounds and words. Everything you did was geared to connect, to grow, to learn, to reach out and interact with your world. And at this point, it was *your* world. That was the only perspective you knew and it was healthy and right for this stage of your life.

For the first eighteen months of life, the right brain dominates. The right brain is the seat of your inner life, your emotional life, and your private life. The emotional aspects of the right brain play a role in attachment to caregivers. Right brain controls and is influenced by the left side. Years ago I read that women hold infants on women's left side 80 percent of the time. In doing so, information goes in the left ear and eye of the infant, which is processed in the right brain. Women instinctively do what is developmentally needed by the infant. Interestingly, men, after becoming fathers, do the same; prior to becoming fathers, men make no distinction on which side they hold the child.

Developmental Focus: Attachment

During this period of time, adult interactions with the child stimulate brain connections between the emotional center and the part of the brain later connected with judgment and self-control. Healthy parent-child interaction results in massive connections between these neurons. The infant has two primary states: contented or distressed. The caregiver's consistent and predictable presence aides the child in learning that the universe is soothing, nurturing, and trustworthy. A secure attachment to primary relationships results.[1]

Secure attachment allows the infant to begin to explore the world, knowing a safe base is always there. Rolling, crawling, and, eventually, walking includes moving toward and moving away from caregivers. Moving away challenges how far you can go and still feel safe. When it feels unsafe, you run back. It is all a game. Playing peek-a-boo is fun because when you see me, I exist; when you don't see me, I don't exist. Over time, you learn about object constancy: I am still here even when you don't see me. But in the beginning, it is a marvelous thing to be here, then gone, then here again.

1. Mary D. Slater Ainsworth et al., *Patterns of Attachment: A Psychological Study of the Strange Situation* (Hillsdale, NJ: Erlbaum, 1978).

Secure attachment is interactive. The big people in your life start to put language to your actions. You put your hand over your mouth and the adult says, "Oh, look, throwing kisses!" The adult touches your nose. You touch your nose and learn that this is your nose. You learn to make sounds and begin to make the connections that sounds have meaning. "Da da" and daddy smiles. "Ma ma" and mommy smiles. "Ba ba" and somehow a bottle appears. You begin to share, even offering to share your bottle.

God Trusted Women and Attachment to Move the Gospel Story Forward

As noted earlier, YHWH was the first to model trust. God entrusted humans with the image of God. More specifically, God trusted women. God trusted Eve with mtDNA, which would be forwarded to every generation. Eve's attachment to Adam, to Cain and Abel, and, eventually, to Seth moved forward humanity and the gospel story. From Eve would come a Savior.

But Eve wasn't the only woman God trusted with the story of creation and redemption. Women move the story of redemption forward. God trusted women to be part of the story from Genesis through Revelation.

In Genesis, the stories of Abraham, Isaac, and Jacob are incomplete without Sarah, Rebekah, and Rachel and Leah. Sarah is unable to conceive until God intervenes. Hagar, Sarah's Egyptian slave, will come to know the God who hears her cries. Scripture tells us more about Rebekah's story than Isaac's. Rebekah carries the story forward by pushing forward the child to whom she is most attached and that God has chosen rather than the one tradition chose. Rachael and Leah are pawns of their father, pitted against each by choice and by their husband. Though Rachel is the loved wife, Leah is God's chosen. Leah will bear Judah, an ancestor of Jesus. Lot offers his daughters to violent men. God's angels deliver Lot's daughters both from men who would violate them and from the wrath of God that was coming.

Dinah, Jacob's daughter, is raped. Her oldest brothers, Simeon and Levi, slaughter those who defiled her. Jacob remembers their violence when giving his sons the blessing from his death bed. This act of violence propels Judah into becoming the forerunner of the blessing that would come to fulfillment in Jesus. Through Dinah's incident, Joseph saw the impact of sexual violation on families. When tempted sexually, Joseph runs. Dinah's experience influenced Joseph's choice.

Judah has two sons who "do evil" and die without an offspring. Judah promises to provide for Tamar, but then doesn't. Tamar tricks Judah into fulfilling his oath. She dresses as a temple prostitute. He has sex with her, leaving his seal as a promise to pay. Tamar's pregnancy is discovered, Judah (who had visited a "prostitute") calls for her to be burned as a prostitute. When she produces the seal, Judah declares that Tamar is "more righteous than I" (Gen 38:26). Tamar's persistence to have a child produces Perez who is in the lineage of Christ. Her name will be used as part of a blessing in Israel (Ruth 4).

In Exodus, the midwives are told to kill the male children of Israel. They let them live, saving Moses, and ultimately Israel. Jochebed will bear Moses and hide him for three months. Miriam will follow the baby in the basket and encourage Pharaoh's daughter to let the child be nursed by a Hebrew woman, Moses' own mother. Later, Miriam will be a prophetess.

Rahab is an innkeeper in Jericho. When Joshua sends out spies to reconnoiter, Rahab protects them out of a fear of YHWH. She gives them an important piece of information: "I know that the LORD has given you this land and that a great fear of you has fallen on us, so that all who live in this country are melting in fear because of you" (Josh 2:8). Israel's disbelief of the spies' report does not negate her role. She asks to be spared when the Israelites conquer Jericho. Her request is granted and she, too, becomes an ancestress of Jesus.

In Judges, Deborah leads Israel. Jael delivers Israel by killing the opposition leader. Before the male trilogy of Samuel, Saul, and David is a female trilogy: the slain concubine, Ruth, and Hannah. Judges ends with the despicable treatment of a concubine. She is raped and murdered. Her master further desecrates her by cutting her up and sending her pieces to the tribes of Israel, a new low in the treatment of women.

Ruth is an outsider to the house of Israel. She is widowed and childless. She is attached to her mother-in-law, Naomi, and chooses to follow Naomi, and Naomi's God. Ruth becomes the great-grandmother of King David, in the lineage of Christ.

Hannah is a childless married woman. She is misunderstood—accused of being drunk when in anguish over her childlessness. Hannah will birth Samuel, who will ultimately crown the boy David as king.

Abigail is married to the brutal Nabal. David had protected Nabal and wants payment for that protection in the form of food for himself and his troops. Nabal rebuffs David. David is on his way to kill Nabal and his house out of vengeance. When Abigail hears of what has happened, she quickly prepares a meal for David and his men. As a result, David does not act rashly but spares the house of Nabal. Abigail tells Nabal what almost happened and what had happened; he dies of an apparent heart attack. She becomes one of David's wives.

David's daughter, Tamar, is raped by her brother, Ammon. David does nothing. Eventually, Absalom, her brother, kills Ammon and rebels against David. Tamar's rape elicits a family tragedy and God does not shy away from this evil act, even if David does.

The writer of Proverbs (presumably Solomon) writes of wisdom. Wisdom is feminine: *Sophia*. The wise are to pursue her. Women sustained the prophets. The kings had godly mothers (as well as ungodly ones). Esther is placed in the king's court and will bring about the deliverance of Israel because of the kings attachment to her. Her acts of courage will be remembered in the Jewish celebration of Purim. Her courage kept alive the hope of a messiah.

The Minor Prophets begin with Hosea, who is instructed to marry a prostitute and treat her as a beloved wife. The Minor Prophets end with Malachi telling Israel that God does not hear their prayers because they have treated the wife of their youth treacherously.

In the New Testament, an angel announces to Mary, the mother of Jesus, that she has been chosen by God. Greek and Roman tradition had women bearing children of the gods, but impregnation was usually through deception and/or rape. YHWH, in essence, asks permission of the girl and Mary grants it: "I am the Lord's servant. . . . May your word to me be fulfilled" (Luke 1:38). Mary was attached to the Lord. Mary's attachment to Elizabeth allows a refuge for the unmarried, pregnant Mary. Elizabeth is the first to recognize Mary as the mother of the Savior.

The *Sophia*, or Wisdom, of the Old Testament becomes the *Logos*, or Word, that became flesh of the New Testament (John 1:1). In the life of Jesus, the woman at the well is rejected by men and by women. Jesus talks to her. John records that the disciples were amazed to see Jesus talking to a woman (4:27). A woman pushes through crowds to touch Jesus' hem and be healed; Jesus stops and acknowledges her. Mary Magdalene's attachment to Jesus (and other women) has her at the foot of the cross until the end. Her attachment has her discovering an empty tomb. God trusted Mary Magdalene to be the first to see the risen Christ and the first human to proclaim, "He is risen!"

In Acts, the Holy Spirit falls on believers on the day of Pentecost. The Holy Spirit can choose any Scripture, any words of Jesus, or proclaim something new. On the steps that day, God proclaims through Peter the writings of Joel 2: "And afterward, I will pour out my Spirit on all people. Your sons and daughters will prophesy, your old men will dream dreams, your young men will see visions. Even on my servants, both men and women, I will pour out my Spirit in those days." God *twice* includes males and females in this section. The first mention is a relational attachment (sons/daughters). The second honors persons in their own right (men/women).

Acts goes on to tell of Priscilla and prophetesses. In the Epistles, Paul and John write of women as fellow workers. Women have churches in their homes. Finally, God chooses the image of the bride of Christ as a metaphor for trust and attachment in Revelation. From Genesis to Revelation, God imbues women with trust and attachment. The first year of life is designed to learn trust and to securely attach.

Abused by People

Impact of Abuse on Trust: Mistrust

Earlier we used the following definition for abuse: a pattern of *coercive behavior* used by one person to *control and subordinate* another in an *intimate relationship*. These behaviors include physical, sexual, psychological, and economic abuse. Tactics of coercion, terrorism, degradation, exploitation, and violence are used to *engender fear* in the victim in order to *enforce compliance*.

Notice that the goal of abuse is to control and subordinate another using coercive behavior. The first stage of development is to gain trust in a universe. These two goals are in opposition to one other. When the goal of the person using abuse is enforced compliance, the child cannot trust their world to meet the needs of the child. A working definition of abuse is "behaviors intended to exert power and control over another human being that wound the other's body, soul, or spirit." The goal of abuse is for the abusive person to get their own way. The wound at this first stage results in mistrust.

The last chapter listed abuses. Another way of conceptualizing abuse will be presented here. One myth of abuse is that if it is not hitting, it is not abuse. But physical abuse is a relatively small percentage of perpetrated abuse. Murder is the ultimate abuse, but more subtle forms are usually per-petrated first. When other forms of abuse do not achieve the goals of the abusive person, more severe forms are utilized. So it begins with a stare, then verbal berating. This is followed by throwing things (and sometimes sexual denigration). Finally, it moves to physical abuse. Most abusive out-bursts include multiple forms of abuse. For example, sexual abuse can be verbal abuse, as well. Demeaning statements to or about the children would also meet criteria for psychological or spiritual abuse. While some abuse is only psychological in nature (looks, stares, glares, body puffing) all other forms of abuse are also psychological. Verbal threats and physical pushing affect the victim psychologically.

House of Abuse

One way of representing this concept is:

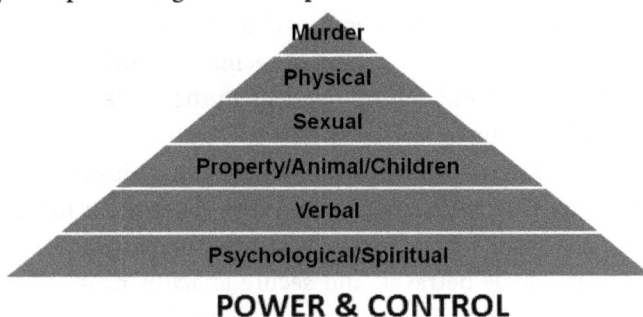

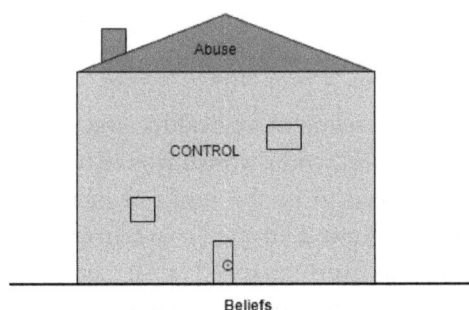

But this is only a partial representation. Abuse is utilized when other forms of coercive and controlling behavior are not effective. Instead of the mu-tual love and respect of healthy relationships, living in abusive relation-ship is like living in a house where fear and mistrust dominate. Wishes of individual family members are subverted to the will of the abusive person.

The belief system, at least the belief system of the abusive person, supports control and abuse.

Mistrust

The result for the child trying to maneuver through trust would be mistrust. Since the first act of trust involved God, abuse impacts trust in God. Abuse impacts the way one sees God. The world and those in it are no longer safe or trustworthy. The world has no order and makes no sense. Inconsistent parenting becomes the model, and God becomes viewed as inconsistent, arbitrary, and punitive. The child sees the powerful as hurtful. Suspicion overrides trust.

My pastor once said, "Both God and the devil get a lot of credit and blame for things they didn't do." People abuse. Interestingly, victims (and others around the victim) tend to hold everyone responsible for the abuse, except the perpetrator. The one who uses abuse is responsible for the abuse. Abuse changes us. It changes our way of seeing the world. It changes how we interact with the world. Abuse happens in the context of relationship and it affects relationships.

Abuse impacts trust in intimate relationships. Those early relationships set the stage for later relationships. When the world is untrustworthy, the mistrust that results interferes with healthy attachment. The child believes that trust equals betrayal, and secure attachment is supplanted by insecure forms of attachment: ambivalent, avoidant, and disorganized.

Unhealthy Attachment

As opposed to secure attachment, unhealthy attachments present in three ways: ambivalent, avoidant, and disorganized. Ambivalent or anxious attachment style is believed to be the result of inconsistent parenting. As adults those ambivalently attached often obsess over their intimate relationship. They can be seen as overly attached to partners. While they hate rules, they control and direct the relationship, often seen by others as bossy. Their needs may change in the relationship and they often expect their partners to anticipate and meet those needs without being told. Their control is an attempt to manage their anxiety regarding the relationship.

Avoidant attachment is believed to be the result of rejecting or withdrawn caregivers. The child learns to avoid attaching, to avoid disappointment. As adults, those with avoidant attachment styles perceive attachment as weak. They avoid emotional closeness and authentic intimacy. They often avoid asking for help or expressing their own needs. In conflict, they tend to be passive or passive-aggressive, appearing detached. They are responsible in their public lives but often lack spontaneity and will avoid emotional attachment in their private, intimate relationships.

Disorganized style is combination of the two previously. This group were the most likely to have abuse and neglect in their history. They tend to see others as rejecting or dangerous. They can be selfish, controlling, and lack empathy. While they deeply desire loving and secure relationships, their mistrust impedes their ability to help build such a relationship.

Mistrust is an understandable survival belief in a world that is unsafe. Mistrust is wise when the other is unreliable, unpredictable, or abusive. This is unhealthy when it becomes a way of life. Mistrust makes us miss out on relationships that can heal us.

Reconciled to Christ

Reconciled to Christ, Who Is Worthy of Trust

When I first meet with a client, especially one who has been abused, I tell them, "Don't trust me. You don't know me. You don't know if I'm trustworthy. Over time, you will know, then you get to decide whether I am trustworthy or not and whether you will trust me." Anytime someone says, "Oh just trust me," but hasn't shown themselves over time to be worthy of that precious gift, *run*! Now there is One who invites us into a trusting relationship. The One who trusted us first calls us to relationship. God understands that we will suffer at the hands of people: "People will oppress each other" (Isa 3:3). The prophet Isaiah wrote: "But now thus says the Lord, he who created you . . . he who formed you. . . . 'Fear not, for I have redeemed you; I have called you by name, you are mine'" (Isa 43:1 ESV). God redeemed us by identifying with us through the pain, suffering, and shame of abuse, abuse on the cross.

Reconciled to Christ, Who Understands Suffering and Abuse

Jesus understood suffering. Through the suffering of the cross, we have been reconciled to God. In foreshadowing what was to come, Isaiah wrote of the Suffering Servant (Isa 53:2–12), who was despised, rejected, held in low esteem, oppressed, misjudged, afflicted, and punished for someone else's sin and pleasure. These were placed on Jesus though he had done no wrong, and Jesus suffered. YHWH could have chosen any image. God chose the image of one who had suffered. In doing so, YHWH identified with the abused, the oppressed, the rejected, and the afflicted as those chosen for relationship.

Once while having coffee, my friend, Ron Clark, explained *tapeinos* to me. He explained that American Christianity has taken on the word "humble" as something I can do by myself, putting on a facade of "meekness." The scriptural concept of "humble" comes from *tapeinos*, with the root meaning of "humiliation" and "afflicted" or abused being closer to the original Greek. Both James (4:6) and Peter (1 Pet 5:5) quote from Proverbs, saying, "God opposes the proud but shows favor to the humble." The one who chooses abusive behavior is exalting themselves and their wants above the needs and rights of others.

Reconciled to Christ, Who Asks Believers to Care for the Abused

The work of reconciliation God gave us was to care for the "least of these." When Jesus describes the end judgments (Matthew 25), his focus is that what separates those invited to enter the kingdom from those rejected was how they have treated the least of these—the hungry, the thirsty, the naked, the sick, and those imprisoned.

Another parable on "the least of these" is Matthew 18. The master has loaned a large sum of money to his servant. That servant has loaned a much smaller amount of money to a subordinate. When the money cannot be repaid, the master forgives the servant. Conversely, the servant throws the subordinate in prison. The story is often used to pressure victims of abuse to forgive their offenders.

Let's consider the issue of power and privilege in this parable. The master has loaned the servant a large sum. This implies that the master knows the servant as well as the servant's need and trusts that the servant has the resources to repay the large amount. Others know about the master's generosity both in loaning the money and in forgiving the debt. The other servants could easily have assumed a special relationship between the master and this servant because of such a large loan.

The servant has loaned the subordinate a smaller amount, implying that fewer resources were available to this subordinate. Power between the two does not appear to be equal. The subordinate takes the loan from the servant, not from the master. Again, the other servants could easily have assumed that this subordinate did not have the same relationship or standing with the master.

When the servant throws the subordinate into prison, no one goes to the subordinate and tells him to forgive the servant. No one says, "You need to forgive him, after all it is your fault you are here." They know the master, or if they don't, they at least trust the master's sense of justice. In our modern day, church members often go to the victim telling her/him that s/he has to forgive.

In this Scripture, the servants risk going to the master. They risk the master's ire if the master had favoritism toward the servant. They risk the ire of the servant, who obviously had the power of resources if the master did nothing. They risk and they still go to the master outraged by the injustice. The master then throws the servant in jail, not for the debt, but for the lack of mercy on the less fortunate subordinate.

I will address forgiveness later. Suffice it here to say that God cares about the abused and calls for justice and caring for the least of these. They risked because they trusted. Mistrust says, "Trust *equals* betrayal"; Trust says, "Trust *risks* betrayal."

YHWH trusted us and was willing to take a risk on us. Christ calls us to a trusting relationship with God. Christ trusted us with the choice. We can choose to trust God or not. God calls us to trust because YHWH first trusted us. Trusting God relies on our recognizing that God loves us unconditionally and wants to walk this journey called life alongside of us, allowing our trust to grow in the One who will "never leave or forsake" us.

Reconciled to Christ, Who Holds Us Close

Christ embraced us "while we were still sinners." Jesus held us and wouldn't let us go. Interestingly, one type of therapy for attachment disorder is holding therapy.[2] The parent holds the child while the child struggles and screams until the child accepts the embrace of the parent. Jesus holds onto us, allowing us the opportunity of a secure attachment in a relationship. Unlike the unhealthy forms of attachment, the securely attached child stays

2. This therapy is controversial, and I only use it here to explain the concept.

close to the caregiver out of a sense of love, safety, and security. She explores the world because a reliable base has been established. The securely attached child feels distress when away from the caregiver and knows that, when distressed, a safe haven is available and she can go back to it.

Based on God's reliable nature, Jesus calls us to trust YHWH. The call to us is individually based; "For God so loved the world that he gave his one and only Son, that whoever believes in him shall not perish but have eternal life" (John 3:16). The call is behaviorally based (1 Corinthians 13; Matthew 25). The call acknowledges our weakness and need for a leader; "follow me" (Matt 4:19). The call honors our drive to live (and choice, which becomes clearer in later stages). The call is to a journey, not a position or point in time.

Empowered by the Holy Spirit

Trust Leads to Hope

One last word about trust. Each stage, when successfully passed, leaves the individual with a basic strength to face the world and the future. The basic strength that accompanies trust is hope. With maturity, we acknowledge that bad things happen in life. When we can trust that good exists in the world, hope carries us through those dark moments. God is good.

The Spirit Empowers Us by Giving Us Hope

The Bible has some powerful words regarding hope. Paul ends his great treatise on love by declaring, "And now abide faith, hope, love, these three" (1 Cor 13:13 NKJV). God designed this trilogy of faith, hope, and love as the foundation of life. God designed a trustworthy world so that faith has a basis in truth and reality. God's love (and the consistent love of a caregiver) enhances healthy attachment and trust. Trust produces hope. God trusted us with the image of God in our innermost being and with a suffering servant as our Savior to give us hope.

Abuse impedes trust and hope. Even in this, God did not leave us without hope. Old Testament prophets warned the people of Israel that God would judge them because Israel did not care for the oppressed, the fatherless, the widows, and the foreigners among them (Isa 1:17; 10:2; Ezek 22:7; Amos 2:7; Dan 4:27; Jer 6:6; 7:6; Zech 7:10 ; Mal 3:5). Jeremiah was a prophet who spent forty years telling Israel that their history (sin) of oppressing others would lead to their demise. Yet, in the midst of this, God says through Jeremiah, "I know the plans I have for you, plans to prosper you and not to harm you, plans to give you hope and a future" (29:11).

Jesus quoted the prophet Isaiah in stating God's divine purpose for Jesus. Jesus entered the synagogue and read the Scripture portion for the day. "The Spirit of the Lord is on me . . . to proclaim good news to the poor . . . freedom for the prisoners . . . recovery of sight for the blind, to set the oppressed free" (Luke 4:18). Jesus reconciled us by identifying with us, freeing us from being under the oppressor, and giving us hope.

New Testament writers also understood the importance of hope. Peter connected hope with new birth: "In his great mercy he has given us new birth into a living hope through the resurrection of Jesus Christ from the dead" (1 Pet 1:3). The writer of Hebrews connected our hope with God's faithfulness (10:23) and with a firm and secure attachment to God (6:19). Paul prayed, "May the God of hope fill you with all joy and peace as you trust in him, so that you may overflow with hope by the power of the Holy Spirit" (Rom 15:13). Hope comes from God's love poured into us by the Holy Spirit (Rom 5:5). In Scripture, as in life, faith, love, and hope are a two-way street; "We continually remember before our God and Father your work produced by faith, your labor prompted by love, and your endurance inspired by hope in our Lord Jesus Christ" (1 Thess 1:3).

Hope Carries Us to Explore Our Autonomy

God modeled trust first. God trusted you with the image of the cross at conception. At birth, as life began outside the womb, you gasped a life-giving breath. In that moment God breathed life into you. You honored that gift by living, by engaging in your world, and learning to trust your world. Trust results from attachment and produces hope. Now, firmly secured in a trustworthy world, you look to explore your place in the world outside you. The Spirit gives hope to move you forward and outward. You are now ready to explore yourself as an autonomous being.

3

Autonomy

My heart, O God, is steadfast;
I will sing and make music with all my soul.
Awake, harp and lyre!
I will awaken the dawn.
I will praise you, LORD, among the nations;
I will sing of you among the peoples.

PSALM 108:1–3

Created by God

And Given Autonomy to Explore

ERIKSON'S SECOND STAGE, AUTONOMY, begins at about eighteen months of age and continues until about age three or four. Autonomy is defined as the freedom to determine one's own actions and behaviors; the ability to be independent and self-governing.[1] You began doing things for yourself. By this point you were walking, perhaps climbing, and running away was a grand game. You couldn't dress yourself at first, though you tried, but you could undress yourself, which you did with great pride at your ability. You preferred to feed yourself. When you dropped food on yourself, you were aware that was not supposed to happen but not aware that it was creating a

---

1. My definition here is an amalgamation of several dictionaries'; see, e.g., *FreeDictionary.com*, *CollinsDictionary.com*, and *Dictionary.com*, s.v. "autonomy."

mess. In fact, messes became fascinating. You dropped cereal on the table and wiped it around just as the adults in your life did, at least from your perspective. Your play was imitative rather than interactive. If you and a friend were playing house, the play tended to be parallel.

During this stage, left brain dominates. Left brain is your public face, your thinking brain. You begin to think for yourself. Memory grows daily. Language takes off. Linear thought begins. You may not clearly know the words for songs but you enjoy songs and can imitate the rhythm. Linear memory has you saying your numbers and singing the ABC song. You are beginning to label your emotions, including anger.

Developmental Focus: Independence

"Mine," "No", and "I will do it" became your favorite phrases. You used these phrases liberally. The phrases "mine, "no," and "I will do it" are important and healthy at this stage. "Mine" is an important developmental stage. At this stage you were naturally egocentric. You only understood the universe as having you as the center. You understood that mommy was your mommy and grandma was your grandma. However, when someone suggested that grandma was mommy's mommy, you were certain they were wrong. Everything became "mine," and even things that weren't yours, you pursued. Over time you came to understand that some things were yours and some things belonged to someone else. This was the first stage in being able to have ownership (necessary for accountability and responsibility). Having something that is "mine" will allow me to share and be generous later in life.

At first, "no" comes as a mimic of the boundaries set by the big people in your life. During the autonomy stage, "no" becomes an assertion of the self for self-determination. In healthy settings with healthy limits, you get to say yes or no. "Yes, I want milk." You began to learn that you can make choices "No, I don't want a bologna sandwich. I want a peanut butter sandwich." You begin to get some control of your world. You can choose when to say yes and when to say no. This sets the stage to for you to say no to abuse, illegal activity, or harmful things later in life. In fact, you can choose to say no to healthy things, as well, with consequences. "No, I am not going to stop hitting my sister" leads to a time-out.

"I will" broadens choices from yes/no to other areas of my life. The will is important in choices and deciding a course of action. What may be seen as obstinate by others is a critical first step to self-control, self-determination, and self-discipline. The desire to exert your will will become important at later stages, when starting a project and follow-through will be needed.

Ownership of your things ("mine"), your body ("no"), or your choices ("I will") is a precursor to relating to God and to others. The psalmist quoted at the beginning of this chapter understood the importance of "I will." You have to have a self to enter into relationship. Your will helps define your thoughts, feelings, and ideas that you will share with others as you share yourself. Body awareness enables you to physically interact with others in loving and kind ways. Owning things enables you to share things with others. All of these have their beginnings in this wonderful stage.

Since you can say "no" and "I will" you can make choices. Over time you learn that choices have consequences, both positive and negative. With this growing knowledge, you can learn, decide, change your mind and make different choices. This is growth.

Because you trust the world to be generally reliable and trustworthy, you can separate and still feel love. You are proud of your independence. You aren't quite ready to give back yet, that will come with future stages, but you can follow directions. Your "no" is testing the waters of autonomy, not rebellion. At this stage, good and bad make as much sense to you as someone speaking a foreign language. You understand that you get timeouts for certain behavior, but the behavior gets a consequence independent of good or bad. Timeouts follow hitting in the same way that 2 follows 1 and B follows A. You are independent.

God and Autonomous Women

God talks independently to autonomous women. The first woman that God talks to independently is a runaway slave alone in a wilderness: Hagar. Hagar is a good example of autonomy in spite of circumstances. We know little of Hagar's history. She was Egyptian and she was a slave. A fair assumption is that she was acquired on one of Abraham and Sarah's travels into Egypt. Remember Abraham in Egypt? Abraham feared for his life and passed Sarah off as his sister rather than his wife. Pharaoh took Sarah and treated Abraham with favor because of her. God protected Sarah from sexual violation and, as payment for any possible offense, Pharaoh gave Abraham many gifts, including male and female slaves. Hagar may well have been one of those slaves.

What an irony, God protects Sarah from sexual violation. Then, instead of waiting on God's timing, Sarah and Abraham conspire for him to have sex with Hagar in order to produce a child. In modern terminology, this would be sex trafficking. Hagar must have had some admirable traits for her to be chosen. The goal was to provide Abraham with an heir. Abraham and Sarah had many slaves, including female slaves. Why Hagar? Certainly even then they recognized that children looked like their parent(s), so I suspect looks played a role. Certainly she was young, Sarah's advanced age was one of the reasons they considered this alternative option. If she had been a slave in Pharaoh's household, she probably was skilled in some area. It is unlikely that she was asked. In fact, Sarah never says her name, only referring to Hagar as "a slave girl," and Abraham agrees (Gen 16:2). Hagar was to be Abraham's second wife (v. 3) with the privileges and rights of a wife.

Once pregnant, Hagar is mistreated by Sarah and, in an act of autonomy, flees. A single, pregnant female alone in the wilderness must have been harrowing. Hagar was probably heading back to Egypt, where she had been treated better. As a runaway slave (doubtful people would have believed she was now Abraham's wife) she faced hardship. The Angel of the Lord intervenes and promises Hagar that she will have many descendants. Hagar exclaims, "I have now seen the One who sees me." This is the first time in Scripture that God speaks with a female independently from a male presence; it is not the last.

Hagar returns. She gives birth to Ishmael. The child grows, undoubtedly loved by his mother and father, if not by his stepmother. Ishmael is circumcised with Abraham when his father begins this rite. Hagar and Ishmael are with Abraham when Sodom and Gomorrah are destroyed. They must have seen Abraham's distress over the destruction. They are with Abraham when the tribe returns to Egypt and Abraham claims, for a second time, that Sarah is his sister. Abraham traveling with a beautiful sister but no wife would have seemed odd. Hagar and Ishmael in the role of wife and son would have helped pass off the deception that Sarah was Abraham's sister.

Hagar and Ishmael would have known that Sarah laughed when she heard she would bear a child in her old age. They would have been there when Isaac was born and named Isaac, which means "he laughs." Ishmael must have been confused when he got in trouble for laughing at Isaac and then sent into the desert with his mother. Abraham gave them water and food and sent them away. Hagar "went on her way" (Gen 21:14).

God had promised Hagar in Genesis 16 that she would have numerous descendents, but here, about 16 years later, alone with her son in the desert, she doubts that promise. When the food and water run out, Hagar places her son in what shade she can find. Saying, "I cannot watch the boy die," Hagar goes a short distance and, once alone, cries. God hears her cry, provides for water in the wilderness. God promises to make her descendants numerous.

Independently, women make up many "firsts" in the Bible. The first to know that God was going to be borne by the Holy Spirit was Mary. Mary was a teenager who, in the eyes of her community, became pregnant out of wedlock. She raised a son who understood, loved, and had compassion on rejected women in a society that invalidated women, made them invisible, and/or sexualized and dismissed them.

The first person in the New Testament, outside of Mary, who is given divine revelation about Jesus, is Elizabeth. The first prophet in the New Testament is Anna, an elderly widow. The woman at the well is the first person to whom Jesus reveals that he is the Messiah. She is a woman with five ex-husbands. The disciples are amazed to see Jesus talking to a woman (John 4:27).

The first person after the resurrection to see Jesus is Mary Magdalene. Jesus sends her back to tell the disciples. They don't believe her because she is woman. Yet YHWH still chose her to be the first to see the resurrected Messiah. Each of these women were attached to and interacted with the Divine independently of anyone else.

Abused by People

Impact of Abuse on Autonomy: Shame

Abuse undermines autonomy. Remember that the goal of abuse is to control and subordinate the victim. Healthy self-esteem was described in the introduction as a recognition that you do some things well and some things poorly. The abusive person comes from grandiosity and focuses on his/her doing things well (even when this is not true) and the other's doing things poorly (even when this is not true). When one is coming from a position of grandiosity, they need the other to come from shame. After all, grandiosity is about being adored, and how are you going to adore me if you think you should be adored or that adoration should be shared? Abuse subverts autonomy in order to serve the grandiosity of the abuser.

The impact of abuse shakes the child's ability to gain an autonomous sense of self. By definition, the abuser's behavior attempts to control and subordinate the victim, engender fear, and enforce compliance. "Mine" is undermined. The "mine" of the abuser prevents the "mine" of the child from being expressed and assimilated in a healthy, life-enhancing fashion. In an abusive home, the child has to be attuned to the needs and wants of the abuser in order to stay safe. "Mine" of the child becomes solely focused on maintaining safety.

The belief in the right to say no is negated. Saying no to an offender is not safe. Offenders reserve the right to say yes or no for themselves. Denying another the right to say no is a perfect vehicle to control and subordinate another. This can be done covertly by ignoring the boundaries that "no" establishes. This can be done overtly with an angry response to an attempt by the child to exert autonomy. A more subtle, and damaging, way of negating "no" is for the offender to externalize blame for the offender's anger. Now those around attempt to please the offender to prevent anger. The model the child is given is to suppress the child's autonomous urge to say no in order to please the offender and for the "good" of the family.

The will of the offender silences the will of the child. The wants, needs, or desires of the offender do not allow autonomy. The child learns that having wants, needs, or desires of their own is not acceptable to the offender and believes, by extension, that God and the world do not see their wants, needs, or desires as relevant or important. In place of autonomy, shame and doubt are left.

Shame and Doubt

The impact of abuse on autonomy is shame and doubt. Shame is the painful emotion that accompanies a deep sense of guilt and embarrassment. The person holds the belief that she is unworthy of love, kindness, or consideration bestowed on others. The victim believes that she is so flawed and damaged at the core of her being that *she* is bad. The pervasive belief is that if you know me, you will see I am too flawed, damaged, or bad to be loved or cared about. So the only option is to remain invisible and hidden. Though she may have an admired public face, she believes that her private face is too ugly to be seen and, if seen, would be rejected.

Shame leads individuals to doubt everything about themselves, their talents and their abilities. Again, the public self may be admired, but the private, internal self doubts that she is loveable. She doubts that praise she receives is deserved. She is more likely to believe the praise is just the kindness of the other rather than a true assessment. I have had people tell me that when they received an A on a paper, they could not understand how a paper they wrote deserved an A. Upon reading the paper, they realized it was good. They knew they had written it because their name was on the paper. However, they could not remember writing the paper. Shame and doubt pervaded their sense of self and their sense of self-worth.

Susanna, the Woman Taken in Adultery

Like so many women in the Bible, she remains unnamed, but her story is well known. One way to continue to dehumanize a person is by continuing to see them as a label (my wife, the adulterous woman) rather than as a person with a name. I am going to name the unnamed women. As a psychologist, I change names of people to maintain confidentiality. In this case, I am going to name this woman to give her an identity of her own. A cursory Google search revealed that some traditions named this person Susanna.

Susanna didn't really matter to the men who entrapped her. She was merely a pawn. Her sin wasn't what really concerned them; the man with whom she had been caught in adultery was nowhere to be found. Susanna's accusers only concern was to trap Jesus. The story actually starts the day before this event. Jesus has gone to the Feast of Tabernacles and taught at the temple. The temple leaders were looking for a way to kill Jesus (John 7:1). When they challenged Jesus' teaching, Jesus accused the leaders of trying to kill him (v. 7). The leaders publicly scoffed at the accusation but privately sent temple guards to arrest Jesus. The temple leaders could not find a reason to charge Jesus and knew that Jesus was popular with the people. Everyone had turned in for the night.

Now, the next morning, the leaders just happen to find this woman who was caught "in the very act" of adultery. They do not bother with knowing her name. They do not bother to treat her with any dignity or worth. She is merely a pawn. If Jesus condemns her to death as required by the law, they can accuse him of the very charge he had made against them the day before. They can turn him over to the Romans, because only Romans were allowed to execute and Jesus condemning this woman to death usurped Roman law. If Jesus does not condemn her, they can appeal to the people that this popular teacher is against the law of Moses. The people would surely riot and they could turn him over to the Romans for causing the people to riot (much like Paul's fate years later).

I can't imagine what it was like for Susanna. I doubt her accusers allowed her to get appropriately dressed for public humiliation. Any protestation on her part, if any, went unheard. They made her stand before Jesus (John 8:3). They take away her name, "this woman." I can only imagine the scorn in their voice and the contempt in their eyes. I wonder how Susanna endured being roughly manhandled. Susanna heard the charge: "Adultery." Susanna heard the sentence: "Death." I wonder if she recognized the man who was asked to judge her. What did Susanna think as that man stooped and wrote in the sand. Did she know what he wrote? Did it make sense to her?

Finally, the pronunciation, "Let any one of you who is without sin be the first to throw a stone at her." That must have sounded like a death sentence to her. She knew she was a sinner and her accusers were respected teachers of the law and religious leaders. Susanna must have wondered who would throw the first stone. Would he be young or old? A teacher or a religious leader? I wonder if she stood there with her eyes closed not wanting to see what would happen. But nothing happened. I imagine at some point her feelings of shame were replaced with confusion. The only man left was the one who had judged her. What would he do?

Reconciled to Christ

Jesus' Musings in the Sand

Many theories exist about what Jesus did in the sand. Some believe that Jesus wrote the sins of the accusers. As each accuser saw their own sin written in the sand, they walked away. Some believe that the woman was naked, and Jesus merely doodled to divert eyes from her to him. Some believe that Jesus wrote the names of those standing around. Some think only Susanna saw what was written; some think everyone present saw.

I am actually less interested in what Jesus wrote than what Jesus was thinking. I imagine Jesus recalled the first time God knelt on the adamah (earth) and created Adam. God's first declaration that something was "not good" was that Adam was alone and so God created Eve. God desired oneness and harmony between Adam and Eve, between man and woman, between men and women. Now here the incarnate God stood in the midst of disharmony, of accusations, of hatred. The Living Water was asked to proclaim death. Truth was asked to collude with half truth (only the woman had been taken contrary to the law). Jesus knew that because of him the accusers had taken and humiliated Susanna. Jesus knew she was merely a tool, an object, a pawn used to find a reason to accuse Jesus. Yes, Susanna had sinned, and so had her accusers. Jesus knew Susanna and her accusers were sinners that Jesus came to redeem.

Jesus Honors Autonomy and Choice

Jesus' only public statement honors the autonomy and choice of the accusers. Jesus did not say, "Hey, guys, I know you all have sinned and I know what sin you did." He left each to examine his own heart: "Let any one of you who is without sin throw the first stone." Whether the accusers left because they saw their sin written in the sand or their own hearts accused them, we may never know. Either way, one by one the accusers chose to leave.

Jesus addressed those with power first. His public statement was to the accusers. They held power over themselves and Susanna. They had dragged her here; she hadn't dragged them here. Jesus addressed the issue not the topic. The topic was some woman caught in an adulterous act. The issue was abuse of power and the dehumanization by that power against God's daughter. The issue was that everyone standing there, except Jesus, had sinned. Jesus was the only one who could meet the criteria set and Jesus didn't pick up a stone. Jesus stooped and wrote in the sand. The topic was death; the issue was redemption.

Jesus Addresses Susanna

I wonder at what point Susanna realized she was not going to die, at least not that day. Now with only Susanna and Jesus present, Jesus rises and talks with her privately. Jesus starts the conversation. "Where are they?" A man had never asked Susanna her opinion before, so she assumes he is talking to himself. She remains silent. Jesus reframes the question from asking her opinion to one more comfortable for her, a factual question: "Has no one condemned you?" Timidly, Susanna offers, "No one, sir," because Jesus is still there and Jesus could still condemn. She does not yet know Jesus' verdict. Then those freeing words, "Neither do I condemn you." He does admonish her to leave her life of sin. According to tradition, she became a convert and, after the resurrection, followed James to Spain.

Empowered by the Holy Spirit

Autonomy Results in Willpower and Self-Control

While trust leads to hope, autonomy enables willpower and self-control. "Mine," "I will," and "no" are necessary in order to have an opinion, a sense of self, and, ultimately, an individual identity. At this stage, willpower begins. Healthy development starts with a strong will, which leads to asserting willpower and, with maturation, self-control. Willpower calls us to live life, to make choices, and to take responsibility for ourselves. As our choices have consequences, life (and healthy parenting) allows us to learn self-efficacy. Some of our behaviors will have negative outcomes and we learn to change our behavior. We learn self-control. This can only happen if we have choices.

Many scriptural mandates involved choice. Moses encouraged Israel to "choose life" (Deut 30:19). Joshua challenged Israel to "choose for yourselves this day who you will serve" (24:15). In Proverbs the wise choose fear of the Lord (1:9), non-violence (3:31), and instruction (8:10).

The Spirit's Call to the Will Results in the Fruit of Self-Control

The Spirit empowers us to choose (Phil 2:12–13). Choice is an exertion of the will. Women in Scripture declare "I will" to express self-determination, praise, and dedication to a cause. When asked if she will return with Abraham's slave to become Isaac's wife, Rebekah responds with "I will." Barak asks the judge Deborah to go with him to battle and she responds, "I will" (Judg 4:22). Ruth decides to follow Naomi, "I will go where you go." Ruth chooses to accept Naomi's God and people as her own God and people. God rewards Ruth by incorporating her into the lineage of Christ.

Leah declares, "I will praise the Lord," and names her son Judah (the forefather of Jesus), which is a variation of the word "praise" (Gen 29:35). This attitude continues throughout Scripture, culminating in Elizabeth and Mary the mother of Jesus echoing this sentiment. Mary exclaims, "My souls glorifies the Lord!" (Luke 1:46).

C.A.R.E.

Hannah vows to dedicate her son, Samuel, to the Lord (1 Sam 1:11) with the words "I will." Other women commit to a cause. Committed to the safety of her household, Abigail instructs others to lead the way to David and "I will follow" (1 Sam 25:19). She defies her husband, appeases David, and prevents the slaughter of her household. Esther determines, "I will go to the king and if I perish, I perish" (Esth 4:16); she prevents the slaughter of Israel.

The autonomy stage successfully traversed, you choose when to say yes and when to say no. You declare your independence. You understand your body and soul are yours. You get to exert your will, including the exertion of self-control. Empowered by the fruit of the Spirit (Gal 5:23), self-control grows. The dual prongs of self-control and willpower set the stage to exert initiative.

4

Initiative

For it is God who works in you
to will and to act in order to fulfill his good purpose.

PHILIPPIANS 2:13

Created by God

To Exert Initiative

ERIKSON'S THIRD STAGE, INITIATIVE, beginning around three or four years old, continues though about age six. Initiative is the ability to plan and follow through with a project. Where autonomy played a role in will, initiative plays a major role in "to act" or "to do." After learning you could do things on your own, you became more interested in interacting in your world in meaningful ways.

In play, you explored the boundaries between yourself and others, between imagination that was reality based or fantasy based. You began to use your imagination and invited others to engage in fantasy and play. Imagination allows you to see things as they might be. Your hairbrush became a microphone as you belted out your favorite song. You were not merely trying on new clothes; you were a *model* striking a pose in your new outfit. The playroom was a pool you swam across to get to daddy. You reached to daddy so he could pull you out of the water before you drowned.

Imagination allows you to practice interactive skills. Previously you mimicked what you saw and played parallel to others' play; in this stage. play becomes interactive. "Mommy, let's go to the park." "Daddy, push me higher." In utilizing preliminary leadership skills, you began to develop skills related to planning, goal setting, and follow-through: "Papa, can we go to the park? Then we can play on the swings. Then I can go down the slide. Then we can get ice cream on the way home. . . . Can we go now?" When Papa says "later," you remember and later ask, "Can we go now?"

Imagination helps you expand your world as you incorporate others. You led in play and other activities. You learned to cooperate. You made a play phone call to mommy who was sitting next to you on the couch. You made up an impromptu conversation. Mommy played along and you took this conversation quite seriously. Later, Mommy said you had to pick up your toys before bed and you picked up toys. Your friend played dolls and you shared doll clothes. You waited your turn at the park because you were understanding that others also live in this world. You took turns on your own initiative.

Imagination will play an important role in seeing through the eyes of faith. Ezekiel is asked to imagine what can be done with a field of dry bones (ch. 37). Then he sees through faith the bones becoming living, breathing people. The Apostle Paul invites us to imagine God's work and God's peace. Then he proclaims that beyond what we can imagine is where God resides (Eph 3:20; Phil 4:7).

Imagination, leadership, and cooperation meld into a vast array of possibilities. You begin to understand limits as well as possibilities. You begin to think about right and wrong. The balance between yourself and others raises questions of fairness.

Developmental Focus: Asking "Why?"

At this stage your biggest question is why. "Why is the grass green?" "Why do I have to take a nap?" "Why can't I drive?" Curiosity reigns supreme. You intuitively know that asking "why" leads to learning about your world. You realize that learning allows you to interact more with those around you, especially the adults you admire.

The most important "why" that you explore is in relationship to others. In the first stage, trust, you were the center of your world and your goal was survival. In autonomy, you continued to be the center of your world and your goal was autonomy. Previously, actions had consequences because the healthy adults in your world understood that was one way to interrupt inappropriate behavior. In the initiative stage, you begin to understand that your behavior impacts others in good and bad ways. Although highly dependent on your parents' values, your conscience is beginning to come alive to possibilities, to others, and to good and bad.

Makeda, Queen of Sheba, a Woman Who Took Initiative

Queen Makeda ruled over Sheba, which covered the current countries of Yemen and Ethiopia. Situated roughly fourteen hundred miles from Israel, Queen Makeda hears stories from traveling merchants about a king in Israel who has great wisdom and great accomplishments. She becomes curious about this king, named Solomon. She has many questions about life, and King Solomon's wisdom is renowned. She imagines talking to Solomon. As a queen of a great land, he would be her equal.

Queen Makeda plans a trip. The trip on camelback will take seventy days each way. She arranges provisions for her and her entourage. Her country has many rich resources that she can offer as gifts. It is known for its gold, precious gems, and spices (1 Kings 10; 2 Chronicles 9). She chooses gifts to show her country is one of great wealth. She considers which gifts are hospitality gifts required by custom and which could be payment for the privilege of consulting with such a wise man.

The planning done, Queen Makeda begins her journey. Each day she mulls over her own understanding of wisdom. She considers which questions she will use to test Solomon to see if he is truly wise. She prioritizes which questions are most important to her should she be allowed only a brief audience. Her imagination plays out the things she has heard about this man and his kingdom. She questions what was real and what was hyperbole of traders. She wonders how she and the king will interact. She wonders about issues of justice, righteousness, and religion. She is a queen, but she knows that some kingdoms are more patriarchal than her own. Will King Solomon treat her as an equal or dismiss her because of her gender? She wonders as the camel she rides slowly treks to Israel.

Queen Makeda and her large retinue arrive in Jerusalem. She is given an audience with King Solomon. After preliminary niceties, the questions begin. She tests him at first. He passes. She asks deeper and deeper questions. The two began to discuss, to debate, to banter. They are well-matched in their thinking. They discuss issues related to ruling a country. King Solomon introduces her to the God of Israel. The God who does not allow any graven images of YHWH. King Solomon offers burnt offerings to YHWH. He explains YHWH's mandate that the powerful care for the powerless. King Solomon and Queen Makeda strategize how to rule with wisdom, justice, and righteousness.

Queen Makeda impresses King Solomon and is impressed by King Solomon. She ceremonially gives him four and a half tons of gold, spices, and precious stones. Queen Makeda returns to her home country, her camels loaded with goods, her mind ruminating over all the things she has seen and heard. Her imagination is now based on reality, not the unknown. Most importantly, Queen Makeda has been introduced to the God of Israel. She thinks about this God who has no form, this God who demands justice and righteousness regardless of status. She takes all these things back to her own people.

Abused by People

Impact of Abuse on Initiative: Unhealthy Guilt

Abuse squelches initiative. The abusive person feels threatened by the child's initiative. Sometimes the adult wrongly perceives the child's exploration of leadership skills as the child being bossy or taking control. So the adult shows the child who is boss. The child never gets a chance to assert initiative or show leadership without feeling guilty for doing so. Imagination dies on the altar of the abuser's ego. Often women will tell me that they don't know how to assert themselves; I ask them when they ever were allowed to do so. Often the answer is "never."

The child's play gets undermined. The adult sees play as insignificant. Dismissing, ignoring, or ridiculing the child's play are ways to subordinate the child in an unhealthy way. Instead of showing initiative, the child learns to be inappropriately fearful of their own thinking and their own wants. Learning becomes "annoying questions." Imagination is "silly." Initiative is "wrong." Childlike plans are "dumb" or "childish." The voice that undermines initiative sinks deeply into the subconscious, rising up whenever the individual thinks of initiating something.

Abuse impedes imagination. Instead of using imagination to see life-giving and life-enhancing possibilities, the child focuses on ways to avoid punishment or ridicule. Imagination loses its value. The child becomes ruled by "shoulds." "I should have done this." "I shouldn't have done that." Reality, with all of its high, low, and in-between points, is replaced with a false surety that negative consequences are always lurking in the shadows. Energy goes into avoiding punishment or making the adults happy.

Instead of enhancing autonomy and initiative, which asserts independence and self worth, abuse communicates to the child that only her reliance on others gives her any worth. Healthy people desire mutual reliance where both partners learn and grow; unhealthy people exploit unilateral dependence and relish the role of playing god in deciding the worth of the other. The stage is now set for dominance and oppression in future relationships.

Guilt: Healthy Guilt versus Unhealthy Guilt

Initiative with the growing sense of conscience allows a healthy sense of guilt. Healthy guilt results when one person has done a behavior which harms another. If I kick you, I feel guilty because I hurt you, regardless if it was an accident or intentional. If it was on accident, I am more careful next time. If it was intentional, I take measures to control my behavior in the future. This is healthy.

Abuse elicits an unhealthy guilt. I kick you and you feel guilty. Now you take on responsibility for my actions. This is not healthy. The most common one women have told me is "I got raped because I was drunk at a party." No, no, no! Rape is not a natural consequence of being at a party or being drunk. A hangover, getting sick, getting in trouble with parents or the law, these are natural consequences of getting drunk. Rape occurred because a man at the party chose to perpetrate a rape. The rapist had other options, but chose that particular course of action.

Unlike shame, which is based on a core sense of self, unhealthy guilt is related to behavior. Feeling guilty for having God-given needs and wants is one type of unhealthy guilt. Needs and wants are part of the human condition. All humans have basic needs for food, clothing, safety, and to love and be loved. Asking for these needs to be met is normal and natural and requires initiative. Expecting to be treated with love and respect is healthy. Unhealthy guilt leaves the person believing they do not deserve to have their basic needs met. Wants are similar. Your wanting something is not a bad thing. You get to want what you want, you just might not get what you want.

Another type of unhealthy guilt is feeling guilty for someone else's actions. Scripture states that everyone will give account for themselves (Rom 14:12). I am responsible for my behavior. You are responsible for your behavior. I may act badly and I am responsible for my behavior. It is unhealthy for me to blame you for my behavior (which is a form of shame on my part). Equally, you are *not* responsible for my bad behavior. If your behavior is bad, you are responsible for your behavior. I choose my response and my behavior. You choose your behavior. Provocation is not justification. I still have a choice even if you have done a bad behavior, and vice versa.

A third type is feeling guilty for behaviors that are mistakes. We visited Italy several years ago. On our first day there, despite severe jet lag, we decided to do some sightseeing. Stopping by a kiosk, we bought a few souvenirs. Later I discovered a one hundred euro note was missing. Tired and frustrated, I lay in the hotel feeling very guilty for my stupidity. As I lay there, I started to think about what sin I had committed, which commandment I had broken. I couldn't find one. I had been inattentive, yes. "Thou shalt not be inattentive" is not in the Bible. I had not been careful; that is true. But I had not committed a sin. I hoped that whoever found it would benefit from it. I had made a mistake. I started to giggle realizing that if I had gone to a therapist to work this out it would have cost me much more than a hundred euros! Thus, the loss had been quite cost effective. I smiled for the rest of the trip. I had nothing to feel guilty about. I hadn't hurt anyone. I made a careless mistake.

A fourth type of unhealthy guilt is when the behavior was the right thing to do. A father verbally abused his child. The mother attempted to intervene, but the father turned and yelled, "I will discipline my child any way I want. Your role is to support me." The mother felt guilty because her church told her she was to be submissive. Submission was inaccurately defined as subordinating to her husband in all things. She was doing the right thing—Jesus had warned about harming a child (Luke 17:2)—but her church's teachings had left her feeling guilty for going against her husband.

Veronica, the Woman with the Issue of Blood

Veronica was living a normal life until that eventful day. One day she was going along on her daily routines and the next day life as she knew it was changed. Her daily life had probably been fairly ordinary. She worked. She paid her debts. She saved money. She lived her life. And then *that event* occurred, after which Veronica was forever changed. She went from Veronica, an ordinary woman, to "the woman with the issue of blood" who was unclean and shunned. After the event, she began to bleed. She waited for the bleeding to stop. It didn't. She must have asked "Why? Why me? Why this? What had I done to cause this?" Veronica went from doctor to doctor asking for help to make it stop. No help came. Before long, the money was gone. She continued to bleed and, according to the law of Moses, she was unclean. Anyone who touched her, or who she touched, became unclean. Family began to avoid her. Friends melted away. Alone, she faced the world. The years passed. From time to time, she asked "Why? What did I do to deserve this?"

Veronica most likely suffered from a vaginal fistula. Something had caused a rupture in the wall between the vagina and the rectum. One of two possibilities was most likely the culprit. The first possibility was that she had been pregnant, and a long, arduous labor and delivery had ruptured the wall. The bleeding did not stop after the customary seven days. Her husband, being a good Jew, would not have touched her while she was unclean. He may have helped with paying for doctors, but after a time, he tired. He divorced her, as she could no longer be a wife to him. The child she had borne twelve years earlier would have grown up without her.

The second possibility is more gruesome. Veronica was the victim of a violent, sadistic rape. Rape victims who have vaginal fistulas, like many present-day women in the Democratic Republic of the Congo, have either been gang raped or raped with an object. The attack was so violent that Veronica would spend the next twelve years bleeding. In this scenario, she bore the unhealthy guilt of the violence perpetrated against her. In additional to carrying guilt that was not hers, Veronica was shunned by those who knew of her illness because they would not have wanted to take the chance of accidentally touching her and becoming unclean. The bleeding would have been odorous and revealed her secret to those who didn't know her. "Why?" she asked, "What did I do?"

Whether by the accident of birth or the violence of rape, Veronica sought help for her condition. She wanted healing. Doctor after doctor took her money but would not touch her. They may have made suggestions or merely told her there was nothing they could do. Finally, her life savings were gone. Her strength was sapped by anemia from the constant bleeding. No money. Lepers had their own community, but Veronica was ostracized by her community. Alone and helpless, Veronica spent days, weeks, and months with her imagination for a full life ebbing away.

Then one day Veronica heard about a healer. She found that the hope in her had not died. It had only gone dormant until the right time. Something in her stirred. Maybe this was the right time. She summoned her courage and her strength. If someone in the crowd knew her, they might yell, "Unclean." Public humiliation would be the least of her worries. A worse punishment would have been being driven away with sticks and stones. The same possibility existed if someone noticed the odor coming from her. Still, this was her only hope. She made a plan.

Veronica knew that no one would touch her if they knew her situation. She couldn't asked to be touched. She had tried that with the doctors. Veronica knew she would have to touch him clandestinely. She prayed that God would forgive her for making someone unclean by touching them. She sought the opportune time. She implemented her plan. Veronica blended into the crowd. She planned to only touch the fringe that Jewish men wore as a symbol of the Torah. She cautiously, unobtrusively maneuvered closer to him. Veronica couldn't help but bump against people. The crowd was so large and so close together. She knew she was risking so much but Veronica was desperate. She imagined what it would be like to be clean again.

Reconciled to Christ

Jesus Jostled in the Crowd

Jairus was rushing Jesus to Jairus' house. Jairus' twelve-year-old daughter was sick and dying. This child had brought so much joy to Jairus and his wife. Time was of the essence. Seeing powerful Jairus and sensing something sensational, the crowd followed. Jesus, the disciples, powerful rulers of the synagogue, the curious, those merely caught up in the crowd mentality. The mass of people took on a single purpose: get Jesus to Jairus' house to see what Jesus would do. Then Jesus did something amazing. He stopped.

"Who touched me?" he asked (Luke 8:45).

"Seriously?" the disciples asked. "A crowd like this pushing the mass of people along. People bumping into each other all over the place, and you ask who touched you? You would be better asking who didn't touch you."

Jesus Honors Initiative

But Jesus knew. All these people had mindlessly bumped into him and each other without any imagination of what could happen. They wanted to be entertained with a miracle. They were not even cognizant of who they were jostling. The mass was just going along, blindly, without true purpose or intent to be changed. So Jesus stopped the crowd because one weak, sickly, fearful woman with initiative and imagination had pushed against the crowd to touch the fringe on his garment. Unlike the mindless crowd, she had intentionally reached out to touch him. Veronica had been safest when she was invisible, and now this man was publicly asking about something she had done.

Jesus Talks to Veronica

Veronica was filled with fear and unhealthy guilt. She had been blamed for her hard labor, or worse, her rape. If she had been a godly woman, she had been told, God would have prevented the event or would have healed her bleeding. It was her fault, her guilt to bear, the doctors had told her. If the fistula had been caused by a violent rape, the last man who had touched her had done so violently. If caused by a difficult labor and delivery, she had lived twelve years dead to the child she had borne.

And now this man, a known healer and itinerant preacher, had stopped a crowd and demanded to know who had touched him without his permission, or so she thought. He declared what she already knew: virtue had gone out from him to somebody. She was guilty of touching this holy man and making him unclean. Now she had to tell everything so he could do what he needed to be ceremonially cleaned.

Veronica fell at his feet and acknowledged touching Jesus. The crowd quieted, trying to understand what was happening. Jairus was annoyed at this woman who was delaying them. The disciples were confused that Jesus was holding up a powerful ally from the temple for a woman who was obviously unworthy of notice. In the middle of the hushed crowd, Veronica began to speak. The whole story poured out between her sobs: the normal life, the event that changed everything, the fortune lost on doctors, the twelve years of suffering alone. She was guilty of touching him, she told him. Veronica was responsible for making this man unclean and he needed to know so he could go through ritual purification. Finally, she told of her plan, her plan to touch Jesus. Her hope to be healed. It all came pouring out. She knew she was healed the moment she touched him. Then she waited for him to respond.

Jairus impatiently stood beside Jesus, frantic to get home to his wife and daughter. I wonder what he thought as the story poured out. The timeline wasn't lost on him. While the rape may have produced shame for him, I think the hard labor would have been more powerful to him. At the time Jairus' wife was birthing their daughter, Veronica was birthing her child. Jairus and his wife had twelve years of joy watching their daughter grow and thrive. Veronica spent those same twelve years rejected and ostracized by her community, without her child. This woman that Jairus would never have acknowledged moved his heart.

Jesus waited patiently and listened intently as Veronica's story came pouring out. Her story was important for her to tell and for the crowd to hear. Veronica wasn't just a "woman with an issue of blood." She had a story and a history that justice demanded be heard. Jesus knew she was waiting for his condemnation. In listening to her, he healed her soul just as much as her touching him had healed her body. People had told her she had sinned and that had led to her uncleanness. They negated her. Jesus was different. She never imagined that anything good was in her. At the feet of Jesus, this healer said it was her faith that made her whole. Veronica had taken the lead in her life. She met Jesus. Jesus commended her. He declared she was freed from her suffering. He wished her peace. And she was made whole.

Empowered by the Holy Spirit

Initiative Results in Purpose

Successfully traversing the initiative stage results in having a sense of purpose in life. You learned to lead, to follow, to cooperative, and to imagine. You thought and planned and followed through. You discovered that "why" questions had answers, and things had reasons for existing. Plans had a purpose; they allowed you to follow a project from idea to plan to implementation, through to completion. Imagination opened possibilities. Imagination allows us see beyond the tangible things in life. Imagination allows us to see what is possible. Imagination allows us to see God. God transcends our imagination, but our imagination allows us to see that something greater than ourselves is in the universe.

During the initiative stage, "I" becomes "we." We lead. We follow. We work together. In working with others we begin to understand that we have an impact on our world. We can impact our world for good or for evil. Healthy guilt allows me to understand that I have an obligation not to hurt others. The fact that I do hurt other allows me to understand sin and a need for a savior to redeem me.

The Spirit Enables both "to Will and to Do"

Paul wrote to the Philippians, "For it is God who works in you to will and to act in order to fulfill his good purpose" (2:13). God has a purpose for you. God wired you for relationship while you were still in the womb, and here you started to give back to others in a purposeful way. God wants you to have a will and the imagination to follow through to completion the purpose God has for you.

Now that you have a purpose, you pursue improving your skills and talents to fulfill that purpose for your life.

5

Industry

Well done, good and faithful servant.

MATTHEW 25:23

Created by God

To Do Things Well

ERICKSON'S STAGE CALLED INDUSTRY begins at about age six and goes through about age eleven. The important aspects of this stage are learning to improve skills and gain deeper understanding of the world and people around you. Play slowly takes a backseat to school and learning. You began to read and had a growing pride in how you could sound out words. Then you graduated to reading chapter books, and ideas caught your attention and imagination in ways that mere letters and words had earlier. Ideas sparked something wondrous inside of you. Books, music, sports, the night sky—each new thing you learned about, you shared.

You were finding pride in your accomplishments. You understood that hard work paid off. While you were able to add to your self-confidence with each task you completed well, you still needed the adults in your life to affirm and praise well-done jobs and offer support and encouragements in jobs that fell short of perfection. A growing competence and confidence built up your heart and soul.

Developmental Focus: Self-Confidence

Play remains an important part in the beginning of the initiative stage. However, play and games move from the free flow of interactive play to more sophisticated play governed by rules and, possibly, teamwork. You began to appreciate winning that entailed skill and luck. You wanted to win. It was also important for you to win because you played by the rules, mastered the game, and outmaneuvered your opponent. Team play also became important. You won or lost as a team. You knew others relied on you and you on others. You could appreciate loosing as long as it was fair.

Your social skills and self-confidence improve during this time. Friends play a prominent role. Instead of play dates arranged by mom or playing at preschool, school provides an opportunity to meet others your age from a wider geographical range than your next door neighbors. You gravitate to those with similar interests, likes, and talents. You make plans to meet and talk. You work together on homework. You have sleepovers, and better still, slumber parties.

Your sense of humor becomes more developed. You begin to understand jokes, double entendres, and plays on words. You learn to banter with others. You talk and laugh and giggle. You gain confidence in what you can do and what you can do with others.

Martha and Mary, Women of Industry and Proverbs 31

Proverbs 31 details many of the traits that an industrious woman does. She is noble and industrious. This is her character because this is who she is and not because she has a husband. Her husband honors her for her character; her character is *not* an outcome of having a husband. She runs her own household and does it well. She provides for her family and for the poor. She speaks words of truth.

Martha is a Proverbs 31 type of woman. She is the head of her house. Her older brother, Lazarus, and her younger sister, Mary, live with her. Martha manages the household. We don't know how this came about: Is she a widow who has inherited the house? Does she have a skill or trade where she earns the money for the house? Somehow she manages a house that could accommodate Jesus and his disciples.

Any inheritance from their parents would have gone to Lazarus as the oldest and as the male. Martha is the head of this house, she is recognized as such. Martha's great strength is in her servant's attitude. Yes, one time Jesus cautioned that she was choosing busyness over sitting with him, but he also appreciates her hospitality. The story of Martha and Mary immediately follows Jesus telling the Good Samaritan story. Martha lives what Jesus had praised in the Good Samaritan story.

Jesus loves Martha (John 11:5). He frequently comes to her house, and she plays hostess in keeping with the role her culture has given her. Jesus knows Martha will refresh him and his disciples with a good meal and a cool glass of water. And, yes, sometimes Martha can get too caught up in "doing." From a cultural point of view, Martha would have been the epitome of a successful, industrious woman. But was she?

Mary, on the other hand, is more interested in people and talking to them. She sits at the feet of Jesus when he visits. Jesus commends Mary when Martha, in her busyness, berates her for not acting according to her societal gender role. Mary has taken the place of men. She sits at the feet of the rabbi and listens. When Mary touches Jesus by anointing his feet with oil, Jesus again defends her when Judas judges her actions harshly. Poor Mary, she does nothing and someone complains; she does something and someone complains. In either case, Jesus defends her.

After Lazarus's death (John 11), Martha is busy in the kitchen preparing food for those who have come to give comfort. Mary sits ensconced among the visitors as they comfort her. Being alone in the kitchen allows Martha to hear first that Jesus has come. She rushes out to meet him. One-on-one with Jesus, she expresses her faith. First, she states what she believes Jesus could have done (the past) had he been at Lazarus's side before his death. Second, she states what she believes he will do (the future). Third, she states who she believes he is (the present). Her faith is all-encompassing.

Her absence unnoticed, Martha returns and informs Mary that Jesus has asked for her. Mary is accompanied by the entourage of comforters and is unable to engage Jesus one-to-one. The more emotional Mary falls at Jesus' feet and expresses her faith in what Jesus "could have done." Jesus weeps. Some say Jesus wept because he was moved by Mary's grief; some say Jesus wept because the crowd didn't recognize that Life stood in their presence. Jesus already knows what he will do. He knew before he had ever traveled to see Mary and Martha. Jesus calls Lazarus to life.

A feast is held to honor Jesus and celebrate Lazarus's return to life. Martha does what Martha does. She serves her guests. Mary does what

Mary does. She expressed gratitude to Jesus by anointing Jesus' feet with oil (John 12).

Humans tend to think in either/or concepts. Martha was good because she fulfilled her gender role of hospitality; Mary was bad because she was lazy and didn't help. Or, conversely, Martha was bad because she was running around worrying; Mary was good because she sat at the feet of Jesus. Both of these are simplistic.

John writes, "Jesus loved Martha and her sister" (11:5). They were sisters and they were two very different, industrious women. Martha was a businesswoman who also fit the cultural view of women who served in their homes. Martha honed her organizational and management skills. Mary was interpersonal but was often misunderstood because she did not meet others' expectations of her. Mary honed her relational and connectedness skills. Mary and Martha had different strengths and weaknesses because they were two different people. And Jesus loved them both for who they were.

Abused by People

Impact of Abuse: Inferiority

Abuse dismisses accomplishments and leaves the child feeling inferior to others. The abuser subordinates the child's appropriate need for praise and encouragement to the abuser's own self-aggrandizement. Disparaging remarks undermine the child's self-esteem. Discouragement sets in. She begins to believe she is incapable of doing anything right. Even things done well become things not done well enough. She compares herself to others who seem to succeed while she fails. She sees herself as less than others.

Justa, the Syrophoenician Woman

Justa was a single mom. She worked hard to provide for her daughter and herself. Her daughter suffered torment. The doctors told her the cause was an evil spirit and nothing could be done. Try as she might, she could not stop her daughter's suffering. Justa had heard about a Jewish healer but she knew the Jews looked on her and her people as heathens and dogs. She thought maybe if she was annoying enough, the healer would entertain her plea just to get rid of her.

Justa found the healer. She watched as he talked to people and healed them. He was one of a group of men but this one was certainly their leader. Justa felt unworthy of approaching him so she yelled at him from a distance. She searched for the proper designation for him. She didn't know his name. He seemed to be a Jewish holy man. Maybe if she gave him a title that showed honor to him and his heritage he would stop and acknowledge her.

"Lord, Son of David, have mercy on me!" (Matt 15:22). If he wouldn't have mercy on her, maybe he would have compassion for a child. "My daughter is demon-possessed and suffers terribly." The holy man did not answer. Justa saw the condescending looks his followers gave her. She saw how they avoided coming near. She heard them ask the holy man to send her away. She moved closer, "Lord, Son of David, have mercy on me."

Then Jesus turns to her. He seems to confirm what she thought he would say to her. He states that he and his people are different, superior to her and her people. But did she see that right? No, she heard what she heard but did she see that right? Was that a twinkle in his eye? Did his tone have a hint of playfulness? She risked everything and bantered with him. She engaged him in word play. And she understood.

Reconciled to Christ

Jesus Challenges Assumptions of Inferiority

Justa had approached Jesus as an outsider. She had believed she would be seen as inferior. Jesus had remained silent as long as she had placed him in a different category than herself. He was Jewish; she was Greek. He was a descendant of David; she was not. He was of the household; she was an outsider. He and his people were superior; she and her people were seen as inferior. Justa had set the tone for her interaction with Jesus: she believed he was the Messiah for the Jews alone.

Jesus' tone let her know he was engaging her in dialogue. "I am sent to the house of Israel." After all, wasn't that what Justa had said. Justa threw herself at his feet and persisted, "Lord, help me." She sensed from his tone and posture that hope was still alive. She moved from using the title "Lord, Son of David" to using simply "Lord."

Jesus Expands Her Understanding

Jesus smiled as he saw her growing understanding. If she was going to assume he saw her as a heathen and a dog, like many of his countrymen, then she wouldn't understand her own worth. Justa saw the puzzled look on his followers' faces. They had seen Jesus interact with adulteresses and unclean women with grace and mercy, but he was acting differently with this woman. Justa understood that this verbal ping pong was to expand her understanding but was somehow also to communicate to his followers.

Jesus used metaphorical language she had heard before. "It is not right to take the children's bread and toss it to the dogs." Children didn't have much standing in that day. Granted, children had slightly better standing than dogs. The difference was that children were in the house. Dogs ate what was thrown out of the house. Justa understood. She had proclaimed herself to be outside the house when she had narrowed Jesus' label to Son of David, implying his mission was only to the house of Israel. He wasn't demeaning her. He was challenging her to think about him, and her perceived inferior position, in a bigger way. He was challenging her to think deeper.

Justa loved bantering and could be quite witty. Now that she understood, she chose to stay with the metaphorical language she and Jesus had been using. Justa understood that while she may have been outside of the house of Israel, she was inside of the house of the Lord. The umbrella she had put only over the Jews was too small. She was at the feet of Jesus. She may have been under the table but she was still at the same table with the same Master. When the children were fed, the household dogs benefitted.

Jesus and Justa looked at each other. They smiled at the bantering they had enjoyed. Justa knew that something important had happened. Yes, her daughter would be healed from suffering. Justa would be healed from her sense of inferiority to those around her. The children or the dogs weren't what mattered. Only the master of the house mattered. Jesus was the master and the house was bigger than just Israel.

Jesus Commends Her Faith

Jesus and Justa shared a moment. A moment of such connection rarely happens between two people. Jesus knew she had gone from believing he was there for Israel to believing he was there for all people. She had initially seen through eyes of inferiority. Now she saw through eyes of faith that the healer cared about her. He had appreciated her verbal skills and mental acuity. He appreciated her willingness to engage him. He appreciated her love for her child.

Jesus proclaimed, "You have great faith." Jesus only gave two people that appellation: the centurion and Justa. Jesus told the crowd that the centurion had great faith; Jesus made the declaration directly to Justa. She was not inferior. She surpassed many of the house of Israel who looked for a sign. Justa had great faith. In this profession, Jesus lifted her to the table.

Empowered by the Holy Spirit

Industry Results in Competence

Learning our strengths and enhancing our skills, we successfully complete the industry stage with a sense of self-confidence and competence. We have the ability to learn and utilize our learning to gain mastery of new skills. Jesus foretold of the Spirit's role in teaching us about God and reminding us what Jesus taught (John 14:26). With this growing knowledge, we gain confidence in the mercy and care of a loving God. Scripture encourages us to approach the throne of grace and the seat of mercy with confidence (1 John 5:14; Heb 4:16). We gain confidence and competence through our relationship with God. The Holy Spirit empowers us to be competent ministers of a new covenant and of life (2 Cor 3:4–6). The interplay between our openness to the Spirit and the Spirit's work in our lives leads to a confidence in God and competence to fulfill the will of God.

Competence Leads to Intimacy

Jesus told the parable of the master who had given his servants tasks (Matthew 25). When the master returned, he commended his faithful servant, "Well done!" Our goal for competence is to be able to do a task competently. Our goal is to hear God commend us with, "Well done!" Confidence in our abilities, understanding our limitations, and growing in our interpersonal skills leads us to desire deeper relationships. This leads to the next stage, intimacy.

6

Intimacy

*Where you go I will go, and where you stay I will stay. Your people will be
my people and your God my God. Where you die I will die, and there I will
be buried. May the Lord deal with me, be it ever so severely, if even death
separates you and me.*

RUTH 1:16B–17 (SAID TO NAOMI)

Created by God

For Intimacy

As NOTED IN THE introduction, Erikson never intended his stages to apply
to women after age eleven. To his credit, he encouraged women to define
female stages of development. Nancy Chodorow, Carol Gilligan, and others
took up this challenge. Erikson's stages heavily emphasized autonomy and
separation, a male developmental path. A male child comes to understand
that he is "not like mother" (mother being typically the primary care-giver
for children) and developmentally goes through separation and autonomy
from the mother. A female child, conversely, identifies as "like mother" and
develops along lines of enhanced relationship, connectedness, and empathy.

As an adolescent, you continued to grow intellectually, gaining confidence and competence with each passing day. Friends became more and
more an integral part of your life. How you dressed, how you talked, what
music you listened to became part of how you formed relationships. You

went places with friends, sometimes ignoring the adults who were there. You stayed overnight with friends and they with you. You shared laughter and frustrations and gossip. You discovered that healthy relationships were mutually life-giving.

Developmental Focus: Interpersonal Vulnerability

For the first time, you began to talk to friends more about your life and family. Unlike when you were two and told things just because you could, now you begin to understand the importance of discretion. You begin to understand that some people are nice and some are not. Some are trustworthy and some are not. Some like you and some do not. You start out with a lot of friends and slowly migrate to a closer chosen few. You begin to explore your feelings with someone other than your family.

Accompanying this self-disclosure is the beginning of empathy. You feel for your friend's hurts and feel understood by your friend when you share your hurts. Empathy brings with it an added level of feeling connected to another human being. This connectedness adds a deeper understanding of empathy, and the cycle continues: you feel empathic, you feel more connected, your personal self-disclosure is enhanced, which leads to receiving more empathy, which leads to feeling more empathic.

Naomi and Ruth

Two women in the Bible who model intimacy are Naomi and Ruth. Naomi accompanies her husband and two sons to Moab. Naomi's husband dies, leaving her two sons to care for her. Her sons each marry. The sons die, leaving their wives widows. Naomi has no way to care for the young women. She is too old to have more male children to take care of the family. Naomi knows, as a widow with no male to care for her, her future is uncertain.

Additionally, Naomi's daughter-in-laws are Moabites, a tribe hated by Naomi's people because of the history of warfare between Israel and Moab. Naomi, whose name means "pleasant," now sees only bitterness for her life. Even if Naomi finds shelter, certainly her daughters-in-law will suffer bitter prejudice. Naomi pleads with the women to go to their own families, maybe some life can be found there.

Ruth insists on staying with Naomi. Like Naomi, Ruth is also a widow. They feel each other's loss and pain. Like Naomi, Ruth is childless. They both know what it is like to be ostracized because of their nationality. They also differ. Ruth is a Moabite; Naomi is a Jew. Yet somehow, Naomi and Ruth bonded over the ten years Ruth was married to Naomi's son. Naomi has seen Ruth's kindness. Naomi may or may not have had a choice in leaving Bethlehem to go to Moab; she was not going to take the choice away from Ruth and rip her from her home and her culture.

Over the years, Ruth has seen Naomi's faith. Ruth has seen Naomi worship a God of justice, mercy, and grace. Something about Naomi's YHWH resonates with Ruth. This pleasant woman had mothered Ruth in the Jewish faith. Ruth cannot abandon Naomi now that Naomi is broken by so many losses. Naomi sees the losses as humiliation at YHWH's hand; Ruth can't leave this old, dejected woman alone to fend for herself. So she follows.

Somehow the two women find shelter, but they still needed food. Naomi's depressed state drains away Naomi's life. Naomi instructs Ruth in the Jewish concept of gleaning. Industrious, relational Ruth goes to find a field to glean. Ruth asks permission to glean so that her actions are understood as gleaning and not misconstrued as a Moabite stealing from the owner of the field. She works hard. She gleans, grateful for the kindness of the field's owner.

Ruth shares with Naomi the bounty of the grain. More importantly, she shares the kindness of the owner of the property. In this, Naomi sees YHWH's goodness and knows that Naomi has not been left abandoned by YHWH. The women work together to claim Naomi's kinsman redeemer rights and a provider for Ruth. We all know how the story ends, but for our purposes, the important part is that Ruth and Naomi have shared an intimate, mutually empathic, and connected relationship. They have shared their lives, their sorrows, their joys, their losses, and their accomplishments.

Abused by People

Impact of Abuse: Isolation

Often women who come to my office have been in long-term marriages. And they are lonely. Instead of intimacy with its mutual give-and-take, they have been in marriages where they have given. Given to their children, to their husbands, to their churches. They have not wanted to bother others with their concerns. And their children, their husbands, their churches have taken. Depleted and depressed, these women sit in my office. Usually emotionally flat. I have been amazed how a simple word of kindness or empathy bursts a dam of pain and sadness, and years of isolation flood the room.

Isolation is a common tactic of men who abuse. Before a woman gets into a relationship with this type of man, she has family, friends, a job, and a social network through her church. Over time, she slowly distances herself from each, usually at the behest of the abusive partner. He claims that she is to "cleave" to him. As such, her time with family and friends impedes their time as a couple. He decides that she does not need to work because he will support her. So she loses her social network at work. He decides the pastor isn't rightly preaching the whole word of God. So she stops going to her church. Or her church preaches that she is to be submissive without addressing abuse and oppression. Her church reinforces her husband's power to decide for her.

Photini

Photini was isolated and alone despite living in a town. She had been beautiful once. That was all she had to offer her world. Because she was beautiful, men had used and then discarded her. They found some reason to divorce her, which was quite simply saying to her "I divorce you" three times. Her beauty, though, attracted other men. Divorce was a privilege of men, so she did not divorce them, even the abusive ones. They divorced her.

"It's probably my mouth," she told herself one day. She had liked talking to men, not in a sexual way, just talking. She liked talking about politics and religion. She liked listening and asking questions. She knew the difference between the theology of her people, the Samaritans, and the neighboring people, the Jews. She was curious how a people who lived so close together and had so much history in common could have so much disdain for each other. Still, she decided, it had been her outspoken manner that had led five men to divorce and abandon her.

Photini was older now. Her beauty had faded. She could work though. She could keep house. The other woman shunned her, so Photini found ways around being humiliated by others. One way was to gather the household water at noon when the sun was high and others stayed away from the well. That, she found, worked well. Until that one day.

As always, Photini was hypervigilant on her walk to the well. She was alert in case she had to duck a rock or avoid being spit on. Since she had been married so many times, the women assumed she was after their husbands and could be quite vicious in their tone and language. The children mimicked what they heard their parents say about her; she knew the children did not understand the words they were using, but the words still stung. Generally the older men publicly avoided her, though some had privately propositioned her. The younger men sneered and either showed their religious fervor or their hormones in their treatment of her. People were not safe for Photini.

Instead of the well being abandoned, a man, obviously Jewish from his clothing, was sitting on the wall around the well. Maybe this Jew would claim the well was his, since the well had been built by the Jewish patriarch Jacob. Photini hesitated. Should she leave and come back later? Should she push her way through? Here's another man making her life difficult. She had been humiliated enough. It was her time to get water and she was going to do it.

Photini approached the well. Without saying a word, she took the jar off her head and lowered it into the well. She was sure this Jew would ignore her and pretend she didn't exist. Or he might look at her with disdain at how she had invaded his reverie and move away so as not to be touched by her. What she did not expect was for him to talk to her.

Reconciled to Christ

Christ Recognizes Need for One-to-One Audience

Jesus stopped at a well. It was a well like so many in every small and large town they walked through. The disciples barely noticed it. Like other times, Jesus sent his disciples way while he stayed behind. This time he sent them for food. They probably surmised he was tired and wanted to rest. Perhaps Jesus stayed behind to pray by himself, they had seen him do that, too. I wonder what they would have done had he said to them, "Go on, now, fellows. I want to talk to Photini. She's a Samaritan woman who has been divorced five time. She's lonely, and I need to talk to her. A group of men will scare her off, so you guys go do something, like find lunch." They would have be shocked, but that was what Jesus planned.

Jesus watched the disciples trail off. He ran his hand over the stone wall of the well. The well was hewn by Jacob, but the plot of land had been given to Joseph. Jesus thought of Jacob and of Joseph. Joseph's children were Jewish (through Joseph) and Egyptian (through their mother). The blessing YHWH had given Abraham, Isaac, and Jacob passed on to Joseph's children and through them to the whole world. The Jews and the Samaritans thought in terms of "either/or." Jesus thought in terms of "both/and." In Joseph's children, the blessing came to both the Jews and the Gentiles. In Jesus, God came to both the Jews and the Gentiles.

Jesus noticed the woman approaching. He saw her avoid eye contact, so she didn't know he was looking at her. Softly he made his request, "Will you give me a drink of water?" Photini froze, not sure she had heard correctly. This man had made a request, not a demand, not an insult, but a simple request. In that request, he put her in the position of power, something no man had ever done. She could say no.

Photini only had her jar. Jews would not eat from the same plate as a Samaritan or drink from the same cup. This man was clearly a Jew and she was clearly a Samaritan and a Samaritan woman at that. But Jesus knew he had found common ground. He wanted a drink of water to quench the thirst of his body; she wanted human connection to quench the thirst of her soul. He presented a riddle. Intrigued, Photini continued the dialogue. If this man can make her work easier, she was open to that. But Jesus had a more important mission than word games or easing her workload. He needed her to understand "both/and."

Christ Accepts the One Who Is Rejected

Jesus now interjects propriety into the situation. Culture deemed it was not proper for him to speak to her without her husband present. He knew culture and he knew her. He would give her the gift of the water, but she would need her husband's permission, according to her culture. His words, said in the kindest of tones, felt like a missile to her soul.

The source of Photini's humiliation was now center stage. She paused, lowered her eyes, and sought for an answer that was true without revealing too much. "I have no husband," she replied. She waited for his reply. What would he do now that he knew she was an unmarried Samaritan woman. At her age, surely, he would have suspected something was amiss.

Jesus revealed the truth about her and about him. He knew more than she told. He knew she was telling the truth as far as she was saying. He knew she had been married five times. For years, I read this as a "gotcha" moment: Jesus says to Photini, "Gotcha, I know the truth about you!" My "gotcha" interpretation was wrong. When Jesus told Photini about her relationship history, his tone communicated love, empathy, and connection.

Jesus said to Photini, "I know you have had five husband." Jesus knew the culture. He knew that only men were allowed to divorce. Divorce would not have been an option for Photini. She had been abandoned by men who were supposed to love, nurture, and support her in intimate relationship.

Jesus said to Photini, "I know the man you now have is not your husband." Jesus knew Photini had limited options. Women were not given opportunities for education or economic advancement. Women had to rely on men to provide for them. Women had no choice. If a man chose to marry a woman, her father decided if she would marry or not. If a woman could not find a man who would marry her, her choices were limited. If she was lucky, she could be a mistress, relying on a single, affluent man who was probably married and able to provide for her. If she was unlucky, she worked as a common sex worker.

I think Jesus communicated to Photini: "I know your past. I know your present. I know that you had no choice in husbands or in their decision to leave you. I know you didn't have options and made hard choices just to survive. *I know . . . AND I am still here talking to you.* Photini, five men used, abused, and abandoned you. *AND I am still here talking to you.* I know the townspeople have humiliated and rejected you and I know why. *AND I am still here talking to you.* I know you are lonely. I know and I am not rejecting you. I know and I am here with you."

Photini tested him. "You are a prophet." Would he accept her interest in things bigger than herself? Would he accept her question about topics that women weren't suppose to talk about, like politics and religion? "What about where to worship?" *AND he still was there talking to her.* Photini had heard about a messiah, and Jesus revealed, "*I am the one who knows all about you and I am the one talking to you still. Now, I am going to reveal something about myself to you: I am he.*"

Christ Allows Himself to Be Seen with Her

Jesus and Photini were deeply engaged in conversation. She with tears in her eyes; he with his warm smile and gentle gaze focused on her. Photini didn't notice the disciples until they were quite close. She was too caught up in the intimate conversation to notice or care. Jesus maintained his comfortable poise, talking to Photini even when his friends returned. For the first time in a very long time, she was not lonely. Someone was talking to her as if she mattered. Jesus had given her what he had promised. He had given her living water, and the dry, lonely places in her soul sprang to life. She was redeemable. She was worthy of humane treatment. She mattered to God.

Photini ran into town. She began shouting with joy. The woman who had avoided attention now screamed to anybody who would listen: "Come, see the Messiah!" The people came out. Confused at first. Then curious. Photini's exuberance overrode their pattern of reviling her.

After Photini left for town, the disciples were still confused. They were confused about why Jesus would talk to any Samaritan, much less a woman (John 4:28). They were confused why that woman would have been at the well alone at noontime. They were confused where Jesus had gotten food after he had sent them for food. They were confused when Jesus began to talk about full harvest fields and the need for workers. And they were confused when a crowd from a Samaritan town approached them, led by the Samaritan woman who had talked with Jesus.

Belonging

Photini led the townspeople back to the well. She ran to the man in the middle of a group of men. In her excitement, she touched his sleeve to make sure the crowd knew which man was the one who had told her about herself. Jesus smiled as he greeted Photini and those with her. Photini quickly repeated the conversation she had with Jesus. Her shameful history now became a badge of acceptance and redemption by a merciful and gracious God.

The crowd convinced Jesus to stay in the town for two more days. He answered people's questions about God. He clarified the role of the Messiah. When Jesus left town, Photini was no longer the reviled woman who stole husbands. Photini was the woman who brought the town to Jesus, and Jesus to the town. Her isolation was gone. She belonged with Jesus, with God, and with her town.

Empowered by the Holy Spirit

Belonging to the Family of God

In isolation, one stands alone; in intimacy, one stands in relationship and community. Isolation says, "You don't belong here. Go away." The Spirit of

God says, "Come!" (Isa 55:1; Rev 22:17). The Spirit invites the thirsty to drink from rivers of living water. Water is a necessity of life and so is relationship. Humans are wired from conception for relationship. Babies who are not nurtured will die from failure to thrive; adults are the same way. Humans need emotionally intimate relationships to grow and thrive. Jesus said *he* would give Photini living waters. It was not something she could just grab in isolation. It had to be done in relationship. She, in turn, brought her town to the well of living water and they drank. Photini belonged in her community. Additionally, Photini became bonded to God's eternal story through the Spirit of living water, which ran like a river from Israel's history (Isaiah 55), through the life of Jesus (John 4), and into eternity (Revelation 22). The Spirit's call to belong is to outsiders: the poor, the foreigner, the widow, and the orphan.

The Greek word for church is the *ecclesia*, or "gathering." Paul's metaphors for the church are always relational: The body of Christ (1 Cor 12:7; Eph 4:12) and God's family (1 Thess 4:10). Peter calls us "living stones" who are "being built into a spiritual house" to be a "royal priesthood" (1 Pet 2:5) and a "chosen people" and a "holy nation" (v. 9).

The Holy Spirit is woven through each of these themes. In Acts 2, the coming of the Holy Spirit on the day of Pentecost marks the birth of the church. First Corinthians 12:13: "For we were all baptized by one Spirit so as to form one body—whether Jews or Gentiles, slave or free—and we were all given the one Spirit to drink." The body is the temple of the Holy Spirit and we together are that temple (1 Cor 3:16–17).

Belonging Leads to Generativity

Now that we belong, we long to see others enjoy that same sense of connection and relatedness. We understand loneliness and isolation, so we look for ways to prevent that for others. Like Naomi at the beginning of this chapter, we look at how to support others regardless if it is reciprocal or not. This comes out of an understanding of intimacy and relationship rather than desperation or self-sacrifice.

7

Generativity

In humility value others above yourselves,
not looking to your own interests
but each of you to the interests of the others.

PHILIPPIANS 2:3B–4

Created by God

For Generativity

As a young adult, your interests expand to relationships in which you give of yourself without receiving immediate, overt, or direct recompense. Intimacy focused on the mutuality of give-and-take relationships; generativity consists of giving to your family, your community, or your world because as a member of your society you understand you have an innate and moral obligation to do so. From birth, others have poured into you: parents, relatives, teachers, friends. Now, armed with all your experience, you pour into others.

For some women, generativity is pouring into the lives of their family. For some women, it is pouring into the lives of people where they work or volunteer. For some, like you, it is both. Secure in your adult relationships, you engage confidently with your children. Sometimes you are on the floor playing, setting appropriate boundaries. Sometimes you are the adult directing meals, baths, and bedtime. You engage confidently with your coworkers. Your years of experience have them looking to you to direct in your field of expertise. You walk into a meeting armed with what you have to offer subordinates and grateful for what others offer you in meeting the mission and goals of the company.

Developmental Focus: Legacy

Established in your career, you sometimes lose sight of just how much your know. You sit in a meeting with supervisors and managers who admire the depth of your knowledge and expertise. You surprise yourself but not those who know you. You help others settle into their careers. You walk with those you manage through professional and personal successes and failures. Eventually, you get that prized e-mail: "You made my career possible!" You allow yourself a moment to bask in the warmth before the phone rings and you are off to another enterprise.

In your family life, you and your husband meld your lives, deciding what Sunday dinners will look like, which Christmas and Easter rituals you will incorporate, and how you will share household chores. Part of this is to keep peace in the relationship, but more importantly you are establishing the memories that will be your legacy to your children. You share your childhood with your children. You tell them about your travels with your grandparents, as your daughter goes off with your parents on her own adventure. You tell stories of making paper snowflakes with your mother while you and your child engage in construction paper projects.

Prisca

Priscilla modeled generativity. Priscilla and her husband, Aquila, worked as tentmakers in Rome. We don't know how they came to be Christians, only that they were and they lived in Rome. The Roman emperor, Claudius, expelled Jews from Rome, leaving Priscilla and Aquila refugees. Displaced, they travel to the popular seaport of Corinth and begin to establish themselves as tentmakers. Shortly after arriving in Corinth, they meet Paul, who had recently arrived, as well. For the next eighteen months, Paul, Priscilla, and Aquila worked and worshiped together.

Priscilla was a close friend and respected colleague of Paul. He called her by her nickname, Prisca, indicating a close, familiar relationship between the two. She and her husband, Aquila, were tentmakers by trade but church planters by calling. Paul names Prisca before her husband, giving her a position of honor, as often as he names Aquila before Prisca. The couple left Corinth with Paul and sailed to Syria before landing in Ephesus. Paul left the couple in Ephesus.

Prisca and Aquila engaged in the daily life of the community. They built tents to support themselves and their work. They attended the synagogue. They shared their faith with others. One day, word came of an Alexandrian Jew named Apollos who was teaching about the Way. Apollos was well educated. He was teaching about Jesus, beginning with the baptism of Jesus by John, through Jesus' life, death, and resurrection. Apollos's teaching was accurate, as far as it went. But it was incomplete.

Prisca wasn't thinking about her legacy when she invited Apollos to her house. She just knew that there was more to the story than Apollos was telling. She admired his knowledge of the Scriptures. What he lacked in knowledge, he made up for in fervor. She and Aquila began to share with Apollos. They shared with Apollos the baptism of the Spirit. They repeated their discussions with Paul, going through the Scriptures, showing how the Messiah had to be crucified and raised from the dead, about the outpouring and baptism of the Holy Spirit, about the unity of all believers. Apollos sat at their table and learned. He took that knowledge back to the synagogue and, eventually, Achaia.

Prisca and Aquila continued to lead others. They had a church in their house in Ephesus. They eventually migrated back to Rome and worked among believers there. Paul continued to keep tabs on where they were and send greetings, either to them or from them, in his writings, which became another part of her legacy.

Abused by People

Impact of Abuse: Stagnation

Abuse limits choices. In abusive situations, the abuser demands to be in the center of attention. Giving that is demanded and coerced drains the victim of life. Creativity is squelched. Intimacy is prohibited. Giving comes from a place of fear and oppression rather than from belonging, competence, and relationship. Offenders will badger the victim onto complying. To stop the badgering, de-escalate the tension, or prevent further abuse, the victim may "agree" to comply. This agreement is an illusion, because only when one is free to dissent without fear of repercussion can one truly agree.

Unfortunately, victims are under the illusion that their compliance was a choice they freely made. For example, childhood victims of sexual abuse who have younger siblings often believe that if they comply with the offender's wishes, they will protect their younger siblings from abuse. Later they remember their "choice" with great guilt, but may not remember their reasoning or the coercion behind their choice.

Stagnation is the belief that one has nothing to contribute to society. Sometimes that belief comes from regret over choices one has made. Sometimes that belief comes from messages received from others that the individual has no purpose or value. As noted in the discussion of self-image and self-worth, the image reflected to the individual is that they are not worthy of being heard, respected, or considered.

Victims of abuse cannot comprehend that they have worth and that they deserve respect and appreciation. When thanked, those who have been abused tend to dismiss the value of their gift. They tend to see only their inferiority and their flaws. They see the negative in themselves and struggle when affirmed. They are more comfortable with judgment and condemnation than with praise.

Hope, the Sinful Woman Who Anointed Jesus' Feet

Hope made choices. Somewhere back before she could even remember, her choice had morphed into a lifestyle. As a woman, she didn't have many choices. Was it because her father didn't have the money for a dowry? Was she a rape victim who was seen as defiled and, therefore, unmarriageable? Had she thought she could do things her own way and followed a path that labeled her as a sinful woman? We don't know. All we know is that she was known to have lived a sinful life. And she knew it. She knew that was how others viewed her.

Hope heard about this preacher named Jesus. Hope heard this preacher was healing the sick. He had given a dead son back to his mother. He had made lepers clean. He healed a paralytic, declaring the man's sins were forgiven. He was rumored to eat with lowly sinners as well as those in positions of respect and power. She had been in the crowd when she heard him say, "Blessed are those who weep, for you will laugh" (Luke 6:21). She knew people were trying to touch him to be healed.

Hope was physically healthy. She didn't need that kind of healing. She had made choices. Her choices had come to define her and she grew to hate them. Hope knew Jesus forgave people for committing sins but she had made sinning a lifestyle. Was there forgiveness for her?

The town was abuzz. Jesus was eating with Simon the Pharisee tonight. Hope knew Simon and Simon knew Hope. She wondered if the preacher's words were true. "Do not judge, and you will not be judged. Do not condemn, and you will not be condemned. Forgive, and you will be forgiven. Give, and it will be given to you." What could she give him? She looked around. Most of the things she possessed weren't worth much. Then her eyes landed on the alabaster jar of perfume. This is the gift she would give him.

Hope made her away across town to Simon's house. She went through the back door. She had been there before, that was how she was able to pass servants and not be stopped. Finally, she was in the dining room. She began to think. Her public lifestyle had been sinful; Simon's public lifestyle had been exemplary. She offered a small bottle of perfume; Simon offered a feast. She was alone; Simon was surrounded by guests. Tears welled up. Emotions overwhelmed her. Fear. Embarrassment. Anticipation. Guilt. Regret. Guilt and regret were the strongest emotions. Regret over her choices, which had led to her lifestyle. The words caught in her throat and all that came out were sobs. She wasn't even sure what she wanted from the man.

The tears rushed out. The damn burst and all the years of sadness and pain Hope carried poured out. She could not control her tears. She tried to dab her eyes and noticed that his feet were wet from her tears. She had no towel to dry his feet. She took her hair and began to wipe his feet. Hope continued to cry and wipe. She feared her tears would stain him with her sin. Hope grabbed the jar of perfume and began to anoint his feet. She sopped up the excess oil with her hair. Hope didn't notice that the perfume she brought for Jesus now covered not only his feet, but also her hair.

Reconciled to Christ

Christ Defends Hope before Her Judges

Jesus accepted invitations. He ate with sinners. He ate in taverns. He ate in homes of friends. He ate in homes of anyone who would open the door to him. A Pharisee named Simon invited Jesus for a meal. Simon welcomed

Jesus to his house and ushered him to the dining room. Other guests had arrived and reclined around the table waiting to see what the itinerant preacher would do. Would he perform a miracle? Have a pithy comment?

Soon after Jesus reclined, a woman well known in the community as living in sin entered and stood behind him. Many guests shared the same thought portrayed on Simon's face. Simon knew this woman. Simon blamed Hope for her situation, and a true prophet would know about her. A true prophet would not let this woman touch him. Simon watched as Hope wept, untouched by her pain. He only saw a sinful woman who began to touch Jesus, and Jesus was not rebuking her.

As Simon judged the woman and the situation, Jesus interrupted his contemplation. Jesus appeared oblivious to this woman as he engaged Simon in a riddle.

"Two people," Jesus began. Jesus started with two equal people. Two people, two debts, one moneylender. Simon was perplexed. What did two people who had a debt have to do with a sinful woman touching him? Simon was holy; Hope was a sinner. Simon obeyed the law; Hope lived a sinful life. But Simon answered the riddle: the bigger the debt forgiven, the more grateful the debtor.

Jesus then turned the tables. Simon and Hope were both debtors, Jesus was the moneylender. Simon offered an invitation to those who could return the favor (Luke 6:32–34). Simon was well respected and held a position of power. Simon didn't bother with the personal welcome of a kiss for Jesus' cheek, anointing oil for Jesus' head, or water for Jesus' feet. Simon had taken on the role of judge who tested both Jesus and Hope; Jesus took on the role of moneylender who forgave both Simon and Hope.

Jesus pointed out that what Simon lacked, Hope more than made up for. She washed, kissed, and anointed Jesus' feet with her tears, hair, and oil. In a culture that valued hospitality, Hope outshined Simon. She approached Jesus as a sinful woman with a large debt; Simon approached Jesus as a righteous man with little, if any, debt. Jesus judged Simon to be lacking and Hope to be forgiven.

Christ Changes the Gift to a Legacy

Hope heard Jesus speak to Simon. She understand the riddle and she cried more. Jesus understood her. Simon's thoughts were easy to discern, anyone could see the disdain and contempt in his face. Hope's thoughts were easy to discern, also, though she didn't know it. The desperation was written in her face. She never thought of herself in the same category as Simon, until Jesus' riddle. Then she knew she was forgiven. Hope had intended the perfume to make an initial payment for forgiveness. After the riddle, the perfume became an offering of gratitude for what Jesus had already declared: She was forgiven! His forgiveness wasn't just for men. It wasn't just for the physically sick. It was for those who had lived a sinful lifestyle. It was for her.

Hope walked out that day changed. She did not know it, but her washing of Jesus' feet became her legacy, Jesus said so (Matt 26:13). She did not know that Jesus would identify with her, as well. Scripture details three foot washings. One was Hope washing Jesus' feet; her legacy was that Jesus chose the pleasing aroma of a broken and contrite heart over the politically, religiously powerful self-righteous. Another was Mary washing Jesus' feet later; she anointed Jesus for his death. The third was Jesus washing the feet of his disciples on the night that he was betrayed; Jesus took on the role of the least of these to show his disciples that they were to be servants to the world, not powerful, as they had been grappling for. He reminded them that when Hope washed his feet at Simon's house, Hope walked away forgiven.

Hope's decision to look at her life, to feel the regret of her choices, and to look to the one who forgives led her to Simon's house. Her choice to wash Jesus' feet linked her to him. He reaffirmed her as the model of Christian service when he washed his disciples' feet. Never again would those present in Simon's house be able to look at "sinful women" and not remember that their Lord had forgiven, affirmed, and loved her. In the story of Simon and Hope, Jesus proclaimed that Hope was the model they were to follow. That became Hope's legacy.

Empowered by the Holy Spirit

Generativity Elicits Care

At the end of his earthly ministry, Jesus instructs his followers to go to the ends of the earth with the gospel. Before Jesus' ascension to heaven, he instructs his followers to wait for the Holy Spirit. The Holy Spirit empowered Jesus' followers to go in service of others. The birth of the church on the day of Pentecost epitomizes generativity. YHWH trusted humanity (men and women) with the image of Christ. Autonomy, initiative, industry, and intimacy matured into generativity to fulfill the mission: to freely pass on to others what was freely given to us (Matt 10:8). We give because we received from YHWH, not because of what we will get back.

Maturation changes focus from self (autonomy, initiative) to mutually beneficial relationships (industry, intimacy) to giving of self to others (generativity). Jesus received the Holy Spirit from the Father, then gave the Holy Spirit to believers (Acts 2:33). What Paul received from the Lord, he passed on to believers (1 Cor 11:23; 15:13). Peter commands followers to use the gift they have received to serve others (1 Pet 4:10).

Interestingly, stagnation is not only regret for choices made (the past), it can result in self-absorption (the present) if the individual does not make the transition to caring for others. The Holy Spirit empowers the bride to carry forward the legacy of Jesus Christ and is the antidote to self-absorption. Jesus modeled service to others; the Holy Spirit empowers God's people for service to others. The Spirit gives gifts in service of the body of Christ (1 Cor 12:1–11) and to draw unbelievers to Christ (1 Corinthians 14).

Care Leads to Identity

Paul wraps these two sections of his letter to the Corinthians around 1 Corinthians 13, the "better way." Generativity results in care for others. It is the selfless caring for another in love, not because of compulsion, coercion, or competition. Generativity sees the value and worth in self and others. Our cultural myth is that we will give to people when we care about them. In reality, we care about people when we go among them and give. Portland has several outreaches to the homeless. "Outreach to the homeless" is an idea, a good idea, but still just an idea and an ideal. However, sitting down with George, who is homeless, sharing a meal with him, hearing his story, understanding his humanity, leads to caring about George. The caring comes after the giving. The giving is the ideal. The caring is the connection to another human being, especially to one who cannot give back in kind. It is innately valuable.

When you can see your value, your strengths, your knowledge, and your gifts as yours to pass on to someone else, you begin to understand who you are at your very core. Empowered by the Holy Spirit, you understand that this you-at-your-core is your identity. Identity begins as a struggle.

8

Identity

Each one should test their own actions. Then they can take pride in themselves alone, without comparing themselves to someone else.

GALATIANS 6:4

Created by God

With a Unique Identity

IDENTITY ASKS (AND ANSWERS) the question: "Who am I?" As women, we develop in relationship, connectedness, and empathy. By this stage of life, you have established mutually intimate relationships followed by relationships in which you gave yourself. Now you look over your history to define yourself. Identity has been building with each of these stages, and it continues to develop and deepen even during this stage. Intimacy and generativity continue to be present and grow during this stage. Identity is the growing sense that you know, accept, and value yourself. You accept your worth and your limitations as part of the human condition.

Developmental Focus: A Holistic View of Self

You see how diverse pieces of your history fit together to make you who you are today. You begin to accept yourself as you are, warts and all. You see how lifelong friends have come in and out of your life but remained friends, and you rejoice. You prune relationships that are draining or unhealthy, and you grieve. You recognize that life goes forward and those you poured into during the generativity phase begin to pull away and ahead, and you accept. You value your strengths and accept your weaknesses. You no longer wish or want traits that others have and appreciate diversity.

Deborah

Moses had led the people to the edge of the promised land. Joshua led them into the land. After Joshua's death, the people of Israel intermittently followed God and fell away from God. When they fell away, they were defeated and oppressed by surrounding nations. Again, God did not leave the people of Israel without someone to speak for YHWH. God appointed a series of judges to speak for YHWH. Deborah was one of these judges (Judges 4–5). She spoke for YHWH as a prophet.

Judge Ehud had died and the people of Israel had fallen away from God. Jabin, king of the Canaanites, oppressed them and cruelly ruled over them. The people of Israel had been disarmed, while Sisera, one of the commanders of Jabin's armies, had nine hundred chariots. The suffering became unbearable and the people turned to YHWH and to YHWH's prophet, Deborah. Deborah was the first of the judges to be anointed with the spirit of a prophet since Moses.

The people asked her to judge disputes between them. They also appealed to her to intervene with God because the oppression of the Canaanites was so cruel. Deborah listened to their plight day after day. Deborah knew who she was. She knew her strength and her abilities. She trusted her ability to hear the voice of YHWH and communicate that voice to the people. Moved by the Spirit of God and by compassion for the oppressed people of Israel, Deborah (who lived in the south) sent out a call to Barak (who lived in the north) to deliver the oppressed Israelites. The geographical distance between the two did not diminish Barak's knowledge about and respect for Deborah.

Deborah ordered Barak to gather ten thousand soldiers at Mount Tabor. On the surface, Deborah's order appeared foolish. Barak had the high ground. But, if he wanted to fight Sisera, Barak had to come down into the valley. In the valley, Sisera, with his well-armed, well-skilled soldiers in their chariots, had the advantage. Barak did as Deborah's ordered. Deborah did not know how God would intervene, but she knew that God opposed oppressors and would fight for Israel. On Mount Tabor, Deborah, Barak, and the unarmed, unskilled armies of Israel waited.

Then it happened. Slowly at first. Clouds began to form. Raindrops started to drip, then the skies opened up and the downpour soaked the ground and flooded the Kishon River. The flood bogged down the chariots, taking away Sisera's advantage. Outnumbered, Sisera and his army fled on foot. Eventually, Sisera ended up in Jael's tent, where she put a stake through his head, killing him and giving the final victory to Israel for this battle. Israel continued to press against Jabin until he was totally defeated and Israel was no longer oppressed.

In the victory celebration that followed, Deborah showed she was comfortable with who she was. "Villagers in Israel would not fight; they held back until I, Deborah, arose, until I arose, a mother in Israel" (Judg 5:7). She acknowledged that the people awakened her to their plight (5:12). She was not afraid to take appropriate pride in her leadership of the princes from the tribes of Israel. She praised those who fought and questioned those who didn't. She gave praise to another woman, Jael, who struck the final blow. She glorified God. "And the land had peace for 40 years!" (5:31).

Abused by People

Impact of Abuse: Identity Confusion

Most abuse we have dealt with so far has been perpetrated on the individual and situational level. Abuse occurs on the individual, situational, and societal level. Situational occurs in the environment, such as abuse in the home, work, or school. Societal is on the larger level of the culture and community and includes churches or ethnic groups on the local, national, and international level. Societal-level abuse includes any time a group exerts power in a way that disempowers another group. The group may be based on race, religion, or gender. Here we are addressing gender.

Messages that communicate that women do not have an equal place in the community of YHWH are societal-level psychologically abusive messages. These messages include headship without distinguishing between a culture that lords it over others and Jesus' command to be a servant. These messages elevate the idea of women being silent without considering the context of the verse and ignore the myriad of verses in which God uses and speaks through and by women to fulfill YHWH's purpose.

This is also done in more subtle ways. When only men speak from the platform, the message is that only male voices matter. Clients have told me that they thought only men's voices counted because that is all they saw in their churches. When only male biblical characters are used as examples of heroes or models for Christian behavior, the masculine becomes associated with "godly" and the feminine becomes associated with "ungodly." When women of ill-repute are more commonly mentioned then women used by God, the message is shaming.

In 1951, Oliver Brown and other African Americans filed a lawsuit against the Topeka (Kansas) Board of Education arguing that segregation ("separate but equal") violated the Constitution's 14th Amendment for equal protection. By segregating children in a racist society, the subtle message was that those with privilege were good and those without privilege were bad. Part of the argument before the United States Supreme Court included research by Kenneth and Mamie Clark.

The Clarks were African American psychologists who had studied children. Their research project consisted of presenting African American children with white dolls and black dolls. Under segregation, African American children labeled the white dolls "good" and the black dolls "bad." Societal racism had been internalized by the children.

When only men have positions and title of power within a church, the message is that men are good and women are not. This message gets internalized by men and women to mean that women's voices have no worth. This is societal abuse that oppresses and subjugates women into believing that their identity is only in relationship to a man, usually a father, husband, or son.

When I ask them a question, women from this faith tradition often tell me what their husbands, parents, churches, or male pastors think. When I reply with, "Yes, but what do *you* think?" they look at me blankly, unsure what they think, and, at times, what they feel. They will tell me what they believe they *should* feel, what others have told them is right or wrong to feel. Without a voice of their own, they cannot own an identity of their own.

Instead of developing a self-in-relationship, identity confusion is a self that is swallowed up by another. God calls us individually to intimate relationship with YHWH; in identity confusion, we hide behind our parents, partners, children, church, or others. We operate in fear that who we are is not good enough or worthy of value. We live vicariously through others. We can get stuck in our role rather than in our identity.

Salome, Mother of James and John

Salome was a wife and mother. She was married to Zedebee, an affluent fisherman. She had raised at least two sons, James and John. She and her sons followed the Rabbi, believing Jesus to be the promised Messiah. Salome's sons were two-thirds of Jesus' inner circle of disciples; Peter was the third. James and John had regaled their mother with stories of their travels with Jesus. They told of the crowds who followed and listened to Jesus. They told of feeding thousands of people with only a few fish and loaves of bread. They told of the storms being silenced at Jesus' command. They told of seeing the dead raised. Although many were present when Lazarus was raised, only Peter, James, John, Jairus, and Jairus' wife were with Jesus when Jairus' daughter was brought back to life. They hinted that they had seen something miraculous on a mountaintop, but Jesus had instructed them not to tell.

Salome also had another important familial connection. She was the sister of Mary, Jesus' mother. Elizabeth had told Salome how the baby had jumped in her womb when Mary had visited. Salome had held Jesus as an infant. She had watched him grow into a child and man. She had heard the stories of Jesus in the temple when he was twelve. Her sons had played with their cousin as children. Mary had married a carpenter; Salome had married a fisherman.

Salome drank in all the stories of the cousins' adventures. She traveled with her sons and Jesus when she could. Salome lived vicariously through her sons. She heard Jesus talking about the new inauguration of the kingdom. Salome saw her opening to seal her legacy in her sons. Jesus had three in his inner circle. When Jesus' kingdom was established, only one person could sit on his left and one on his right. Salome wanted to improve the odds that her sons were in these two positions. Her sons were the logical choice. Jesus, James, and John were family. Surely Jesus would honor an aunt's request. So she approached Jesus, with her sons' approval, to ask that fateful question: Can my sons have those places of honor on your left and on your right? She had not moved from generativity to value her unique identity.

Reconciled to Christ

Christ Has Compassion on Salome

Jesus looked at Salome with compassion. He knew she was asking from a mother's heart. He also knew that her concept of the kingdom was inaccurate and she did not know what she was asking. He knew she didn't understand now, but she would. "You don't know what you are asking" was Jesus' reply. He was not condemning her. He knew the day was coming when she would be the one with an important message to tell her sons.

Christ Addresses the Fallout of Salome's Question

Salome's question had spurred jealousy among the twelve disciples. They began to argue who among them deserved places of honor in the kingdom Jesus would usher in. Although Jesus had been telling them of his pending crucifixion and death, they had not taken the statements literally. As they were preparing for the Passover meal, they surely must have thought how the Passover was God's final judgment on Egypt which led to Israel's freedom from oppression. They wondered when Jesus would rise up against Rome and set up his kingdom, taking on the throne of David. Maybe this Passover would be the time. After all, hadn't the crowds hailed Jesus as king. The crowds had sung "Hosanna" as Jesus had ridden a donkey into Israel.

Against this backdrop, Jesus gathered with his disciples for the Passover meal. Then Jesus did the unthinkable. He got up from his seat, wrapped a towel around his waist, and did the job of the lowest slave. He washed their feet. Two women had washed Jesus' feet, one early in his ministry and one late. But now Jesus was on his knees, washing their feet. They wanted to know who was going to get the seats of power in Jesus' kingdom and here he was on his knees.

Then Jesus began to speak. "Remember when the centurion sent the message that he understood what it was to have authority. He told one to go and he went; he told one to come and he came?" The disciples were confused. What did foot washing and authority have to do with each other? But Jesus continued, "The kings of the Gentiles lord it over them . . . but this is not how I do it and it is not how you are supposed to do it. You are to serve others. Do as I do, take on the role of the slave or a woman who washes others' feet" (Luke 22:25–27, my paraphrase).

Christ Gives Salome Her Own Identity

When Salome asked the question, Jesus knew that she would have her own cup to drink but he couldn't tell her. Shortly after the question, Jesus was arrested. Even that night, her sons and Peter were nearest him and told the story of the Passover meal, the prayer time in Gethsemane, and the soldiers arresting Jesus. Salome rushed to find her sister. Salome could not image what Mary was going through. Salome, Mary the mother of Jesus, and other women waited earnestly for news of Jesus. Eventually, they saw him. They hardly recognized him because he was so battered and bruised. They heard that Jesus had been condemned to be crucified. At the foot of the cross, Salome stood with her sister Mary.

Salome heard the thief crucified beside Jesus ask to be remembered when Jesus came to his kingdom. Salome remembered her own request regarding Jesus' kingdom. She wondered what she would have done if James and John were being crucified on each side of him. Salome heard Jesus ask her son, John, to care for Mary as his own mother. The request was consistent with Jewish law that a male relative care for a widow. Salome had asked Jesus for a position of power for John; Jesus had asked John to take a relational position with his mother. She was moved with compassion for her sister and knew that John and Salome would care for Mary in their home. After John took Mary away, Salome and the other women felt unsafe without a male presence and moved from the foot of the cross to a more distant point to observe.

Salome and the other women quickly made plans to take burial spices after the Sabbath had passed. She hurried home after Jesus was pronounced dead. She had her husband, her sons, and Mary to care for. She had to prepare the Sabbath meal. The family numbly went through the Sabbath rituals. No one could make sense of what had happened and no words seemed adequate. Slowly the day passed.

Finally, the sun rose on the day after the Sabbath. Salome joined Mary Magdalene and the other women to go to the tomb. The women fearfully planned how to ask the soldiers to move the tombstone. Maybe the soldiers would take pity on a group of grieving women. When they arrived, the tomb was unguarded and the entrance to the tomb was empty. The women looked in the tomb. The body was gone. Calmly sitting inside the tomb was a young man, he told them Jesus was risen!

Salome became one of the first evangelists! She returned to the disciples to report the tomb was empty and Jesus had risen (Luke 24:9)! Now she had a story to tell, the story of the empty tomb. She cared for Mary. She drank from the cup at the crucifixion of Jesus and, later, at the death of her son, James, the first apostle to be martyred. She followed Jesus from the beginning of his ministry until the end of her life. She no longer lived vicariously through her sons. She came to understand her identity through her relationships and her care for others. She had her own identity as one of the first to witness the empty tomb and to receive the message of the risen Christ.

Empowered by the Holy Spirit

Identity Leads to Confidence

The Holy Spirit empowers us to speak the good news that Jesus has risen. Unlike an identity based on autonomy and that is self-chosen, identity for women (and, I believe, for Christians) comes out of relationship with God and with others. Our identities are intertwined with understanding ourselves in our living out the gospel of the Christ, who took off the form of divinity and took on the form of humanity (Phil 2:6). In that human form, Jesus took on the form of a servant. This servant stood against the powerful and oppressors and identified with the "least of these."

When Jesus ascended to heaven, YHWH poured out the Holy Spirit on the day of Pentecost. God proclaimed the end of identity based on status and power. Identity now came as a result of Christ identifying with us and the outpouring of the Holy Spirit on believers, regardless of gender, economic status, race, or ethnicity. Peter stood on the steps to explain what had happened. He could have picked any Scripture: Abraham and the son who was sacrificed, the Passover lamb, the descendant of David and spiritual King. Peter could have repeated any of the words or works of Jesus. Peter could have chosen to coin something new and pithy. Instead, filled by the Holy Spirit, Peter picked Joel 2, telling the crowd that God said the Spirit would be poured out on the sons and daughters of God; on male and female servants. The hierarchy of society is overturned by the God who values us regardless of gender. We get our own identity.

Autonomy emphasizes the "will" in "I will." Identity emphasizes the "I." And I am okay with the fact that "I" am an "I." I have confidence in my God and my abilities. I "approach God's throne of grace with confidence" (Heb 4:16) and freedom (Eph 3:12). I am confident that I will see the goodness of God (Ps 27:13).

C.A.R.E.

Confident in Our Identity Leads to Ego Integrity

Now that the question "Who am I?" has been wrestled into understanding, the question turns to "What is the meaning of life?" This latter question is the central theme of the last stage. I have lived, I have given, what does it mean in the bigger scheme of things? That is the work of ego integrity.

9

Ego Integrity

Blessed are those who find wisdom, those who gain understanding,
for she is more profitable than silver and yields better returns than gold.
She is more precious than rubies; nothing you desire can compare with her.
Long life is in her right hand.. Her ways are pleasant ways,
and all her paths are peace.
She is a tree of life to those who take hold of her; those who hold her fast will
be blessed.

PROVERBS 3:13–18

Created by God

For Ego Integrity

EGO INTEGRITY WAS ERIKSON's final stage. In this stage, you look back over your life and move past "Who am I?" to "Did my life have meaning?" We will all have some regrets, but the goal is to have the fewest regrets possible. Since you have accepted who you are, the goal is to accept your life as part of a bigger picture. By now you begin to see the end of your professional life. Your children are grown and having families of their own. You wonder if your life had meaning outside of just you. You wonder if those you touched felt touched.

Life has allowed you to see things come full circle. You started as the child who experienced. You were the adult who used that experience to connect to others and to give children experience and guidance. Now you become the observer of those experiencing and giving experiences. Friends have come in and out of your life. Some have circled closer despite distance in time and place. Some have circled away despite geographical closeness. You begin to understand not only your legacy, but the legacy of your ancestors on your life. You look backward and forward.

Reflection and Acceptance of One's Life

Early in this stage, you begin to move from a professional life to a life outside of the professional sector. Without your identity coming from what you do, your focus expands to consider the role you played on this speck of dust known as planet earth. You know that the time to choose alternate paths is now limited. Your reflections include wrestling with paths not taken and coming to peace with those decisions. Reflections also include wrestling with paths you have regretted taking and coming to peace with those, as well.

You reflect on the good you see in your life. You appreciate friends and family who helped you grow and find purpose in life. You smile when you see your subordinates move into positions of power and influence. You feel humbled when you see your children carry on your legacy with their children. You feel a sense of gratitude. As much as you wish you could have frozen certain time periods, you realize that others deserve the gifts life has given you. You see others make the same mistakes you did and you know that it will be okay. They will learn and grow just as you did.

You wonder about what meaning life has for you now. Time seems short, but you still get to make choices. You can travel or invest in your community. You can volunteer or live a more isolated lifestyle. You see your life has many threads that have been woven through the tapestry of many lives. Those lives have also given the tapestry of your life depth, meaning, and perspective.

Anna the Prophetess

Anna was the daughter of Phanuel and a descendant of the tribe of Asher. Phanuel had raised Anna to be proud of her heritage. He made sure his daughter knew of the importance of women in the lineage of Asher, son of Jacob. Asher meant "happy," and though Asher was the son of Leah's slave woman, Asher's daughter Serah had been a favorite of Jacob. According to Jewish tradition, Serah was musically gifted and had been recruited to tell her grandfather, Jacob, that his son, Joseph, was still alive. Serah migrated with her grandfather and his extended family to Egypt. In fact, Serah was the only woman listed by name and numbered among the seventy descendants that traveled to Egypt with Jacob. Serah lived to a very old age; tradition held that she lived to see Moses and declare that he was God's means of deliverance from the oppression of Egypt.

Phanuel explained to Anna that his name was Greek because the tribe of Asher had been part of the Northern Kingdom of Israel that was led into captivity and dispersed to the ends of the earth. Phanuel's ancestors valued their heritage and verbally passed their traditions from generation to generation. Phanuel told Anna that the women of the tribe of Asher were known for their spiritual depth and their beauty. As such, they were favored and chosen as wives by kings and priests.

Anna followed both her ancestry and destiny when she married a young priest. During the seven years of their marriage, Anna established her place among the women in the temple. Anna was devastated when her husband died. Her brother-in-law, also a priest, was not able to take on the obligations of a levirate marriage. Anna and her brother-in-law agreed they would perform the *halizah*. Anna was now free from the obligation of being married to her brother-in-law. As a widow, she was entitled to the same financial and social support she had been given as a wife. Though she was young and pressured to remarry, Anna remained celibate. She worshipped daily in the temple, ministering to women in the court of women who came for ritual purification.

Year after year passed. Anna fasted and prayed. Her identity shifted from that of young widow to godly woman to elderly prophet. No one knows when she was labeled a prophet, but her inner spiritual life led to public acknowledgement of her wisdom and of her ability to speak for God. Many thought the age of the prophets had passed, but Anna challenged that belief. She fasted and prayed for Israel and Jerusalem year after year. God had spoken to her and told her that she would see the redeemer of Israel.

Anna befriended Simeon. The two spoke about their hope that the Messiah would come. Together they wrestled with holy writings that seemed to say that the Messiah would be lifted up on a tree and rejected. They wondered together when the Messiah would come, both believing it would happen in their lifetime. Anna surely joked that her long life must have been for some purpose, perhaps to witness the Messiah.

One day Anna walked into the temple. She saw Simeon standing with a young couple. She saw the look on his face. She had seen the look before. She had seen it every time they had wondered about the Messiah. Anna made her way over to Simeon and heard him declare, "My eyes have seen your salvation." Anna recognized the Holy Spirit speaking through Simeon. She affirmed his declaration from her own prophetic gift.

Anna knew the day she had looked forward to all her life was now here. She knew she had seen YHWH's Messiah. Her life was now on a bigger stage than the temple; it was connected to the redemption of Israel. Anna's life mission shifted. Up to this point, she had proclaimed the coming of the Messiah. She spent the rest of her life proclaiming that the Messiah had come and she had seen him. Despite her age, she spent the rest of her life telling of the day she walked into the temple and saw the one who would redeem Jerusalem.

Abuse by People

Impact of Abuse: Despair

When one is unable to identify a meaning and purpose in life, life seems meaningless. Sometimes this comes from a life lived without concern for anything or anyone but the experience of the moment. Sometimes this comes from a life lived through someone else's script. For victims of abuse, so much time is spent trying to stay safe from abuse that living a self-determined, self-defined life is missed. In essence, the abuser has put him/herself in the position of God, and now the victim recognizes they have not lived a life of fullness and wholeness. Bitterness and despair set in.

Hope for something different is lost. This is despair. Your reflections on life focus on what-ifs, what might have been, or what should have been. Instead of accepting that life is a journey with peaks and valleys, you experience despair over missed opportunities and isolated moments. Missed opportunities include questioning and re-questioning the choices that you made. "If only" I had chosen A instead of B. The assumption is that the alternative choice would have been better. "If only" I had not chosen A, assuming that one could have known the outcome before it was a reality.

Despair misses the point that to decide is to kill other options. However, without making decisions, you would have lived a paralyzed life.

Isolated moments elevate either times of success or times of failure. This focus loses the "both/and" aspect of life. The times of failure provided lessons which allowed for times of success. Hyperfocusing on either leaves one living in the past rather than the present. Regrets come from focusing on failure; bitterness comes from focusing on successes of others or successes which could not be sustained.

Mary Magdalene

Mary was born and raised in Magdala. Her family was influential and she was raised with the privileges of affluence. She was well taken care of. She had access to whatever she wanted or needed. However, the affliction that overtook her started when she was young and, by the time she was an adult, it completely encompassed all of her life. Then she met Jesus. He healed her. Like so many other women he touched, Mary Magdalene was made completely whole. She followed him and spent time with him. He treated her with kindness and respect. He listened to her and she listened to him.

Mary supported Jesus with her family funds. She supported him with her attention and affection. He supported her inquisitiveness and dedication to the God of Abraham. He was gracious and kind in accepting her devotion. She loved the way he touched the sick and healed them. She noticed that he showed no discrimination in whom he touched: men, women, children, lame, epileptic, young, old, clean, unclean, rich, poor, Jews, Romans, Samaritans, Phoenicians, Greeks, free, slave. He spoke in a way that was so very Jewish and yet so very different from religious leaders, and definitely different than the ruling Romans. Each time he spoke, whether to individuals or mass crowds, he spoke with authority and yet with kindness and compassion. He spoke in riddles, and she liked that.

Mary Magdalene was hopeful that this Messiah would be different. He did not condemn those who opposed him. He did not try to raise an armed rebellion. He talked of turning the other cheek and caring for the lowest in society: children, poor, helpless. Mary Magdalene recognized this as carrying on the words of Moses and the prophets. She had never seen anyone live out the law and the prophets in the way that Jesus did. She could see how his kingdom would be different. Although she believed his words that he would establish his kingdom, she could not conceive how he would overthrow the Roman rulers.

Mary Magdalene was finishing the Passover meal when news reached her that Jesus had been arrested. She frantically sought out the apostles and Jesus' mother, Mary. Mary, Mary Magdalene, Salome, and other women were gathered at Mary's home when Joanna appeared with news. Joanna's husband, Chuza, worked in Herod's household. Jesus had been arrested, questioned by the Sanhedrin, and turned over to Pilate. Pilate, trying to build a political alliance with Herod, had sent Jesus for an audience with Herod. Chuza was there when Jesus was questioned by Herod, and Chuza had sent word for Joanna.

Joanna told the women that Jesus had refused to talk to Herod and was sent back to Pilate. The women quickly made their way to Pilate's courtyard. They saw Jesus standing beside Pilate. Jesus looked beaten and battered. They heard Pilate say that he and Herod had found no justification to the charge of rebellion and no justification for a death penalty. The women breathed a sigh of relief. Jesus would be released.

But then the crowds began to yell, "Away with him! Crucify him!"

The women felt scared and confused. Things began to get out of hand so quickly. Pilate declared Barabbas would be set free and Jesus would be crucified. Pilate washed his hands and Jesus was led away. The crowds followed. Some followed because Jesus was being crucified. Some followed because they wanted to see the two thieves who were also being crucified. Some followed just to watch a crucifixion, oblivious to who was being crucified.

Mary Magdalene wrapped her arm around Jesus' mother as they followed the crowd. Salome, Joanna, Susanna, and John were close by as they made their way up the Via Dolorosa to Golgotha. Quietly they were all trying to make sense of what was happening. Mary Magdalene had been sure this was the Messiah. How could this be happening? She watched as Jesus was nailed to the cross and lifted into place. She was too numb to notice the tears running down her cheeks. She could tell Mary was also numb as they walked through this nightmare together.

Mary Magdalene handed Mary off to John when Jesus put her in his care. She heard his words of forgiveness. She was struck by the different reactions of those present. The religious leaders were sneering at Jesus to come down from the cross, ridiculing his claims to save others. The Roman soldiers went about their work with precision. After mechanically placing the nails and the posts, the soldiers' mood changed as they joked and rolled dice for whatever belongings the condemned had of any worth. One thief mocked Jesus, while the other seemed to show some compassion.

Slowly, the meaning of life slipped away from Mary Magdalene. When Jesus announced, "It is finished," Mary Magdalene nodded. It is finished. The hope for a different future. The Messiah who would invite everyone to live in peace and compassion and justice and righteousness was dead. And so was his work and her future.

Mary Magdalene stood wordlessly as others walked away. She had nowhere to go. No other man had listened to women and valued them like Jesus had. Mary Magdalene replayed all that had happened and it all seemed so meaningless now. Life was meaningless. She and Salome flatly wondered what would happen to his body. They watched as it was lowered from the cross. They followed two men who had taken the body from the soldiers. The men carried the body to a tomb. They watched where the body was laid. They watched as a large stone was placed over the opening.

Mary Magdalene hurried home so she would not violate the Sabbath. Exhausted, she fell into a fitful night of sleep. The images of the day invaded her dreams. She tossed and turned, unable to get comfortable. Once the numbness lifted, the tears started to pour out. They were tears of despair and hopelessness. She could find no respite from the pervasive darkness that surrounded her. The Sabbath passed but without its usual restfulness.

Mary Magdalene, Salome, and other women rose early to put together the spices needed to properly anoint Jesus' dead body. They hurried to the tomb, wondering how they would roll away the large stone covering the opening. The tomb was open. The body was gone. Mary Magdalene ran back to the disciples and declared that the body was gone. She assumed the soldiers or the religious leaders had moved it so Jesus' followers would have no place to pay him homage. Peter and John raced to the tomb and Mary Magdalene followed. She could not understand how a dead body could be a threat. She had watched him die and now she was prevented from giving him the homage he was due. Her despair was complete.

Reconciled to Christ

Despair to Faith

Mary Magdalene was alone at the tomb. She looked inside and did not comprehend what she was seeing. Through her tears, she saw figures but did not know she was talking to angels. She was desperate to find his body. When a male voice softly inquired why she was crying and who she was looking for, Mary Magdalene assumed the gardener was bothered by her emotional presentation. She felt a small spark of hope that she might recover the body.

"Sir, if you have carried him away, tell me where you have put him, and I will get him" (John 20:15).

Then came the voice of the one who had spoken her name so many times. "Mary." She knew the voice; she knew the one whose voice brought such comfort. She did not fully understand, but she somehow intuitively knew that her life was entwined with something bigger than herself. Despair was lifted. She had found his body and he was alive. He spoke to her.

While Anna was the first prophet of the New Testament, Mary Magdalene was the first evangelist of the risen Christ. Her message changed from "I can't find his body" to "I have seen the risen Lord!" Anna was the first to recognize the incarnate infant as Jerusalem's redeemer; Mary Magdalene was the first to recognize the crucified Jesus as the risen Lord. Death had lost and life reigned supreme. Despair was conquered.

Empowered by the Holy Spirit

Ego Integrity Leads to Wisdom

Ego integrity is the ability to see our lives as part of a bigger picture without seeing our lives as small. We are only given this one life. We are to live it to the fullest. We will have successes, failures, and everything in between. Throughout our lives we will grow in understanding the world around us, as well as ourselves. With ego integrity, we gain wisdom. The Holy Spirit gives wisdom to the mature (1 Cor 2:6).

The Holy Spirit inspired the writer of Proverbs to write about wisdom. In Hebrew, the word for wisdom is *Sophia*, feminine. *Sophia* of Proverbs will become the *Logos* of John (John 1:1). This is mystery. One of the interesting things about wisdom is that it knows it cannot know everything. Wisdom knows that we cannot understand Three-Persons-in-One God nor

One-God-in-Three-Persons. Wisdom understands that as limited humans we can only comprehend an eternal, unfathomable YHWH in limited terms, as YHWH chooses to reveal to us. Sophia knows this and accepts this and is grateful for the life given.

Sophia knows that from Eve in Genesis to the bride of Christ in Revelation, the cloud of witnesses (Heb 12:1–3) surrounding our faith includes women from every walk of life. For our sisters and daughters who have only known male voices to define the faith, we present this proud heritage of women who were used by God to carry forth the message of the gospel. For our sisters and daughters who have only known limited images for women (i.e., the Virgin Mary or Jezebel), we present a heritage that is as diverse as our experiences. We have been mothers, daughters, daughters-in-law, sisters, young, old, rich, poor, physically ill, physically healthy. We have led and we have followed. We have challenged and bantered. We have listened and learned. And whatever we have been through, we have been created, reconciled, and empowered by a loving God for relationship and wholeness.

www.ingramcontent.com/pod-product-compliance
Lightning Source LLC
Chambersburg PA
CBHW070515090426
42735CB00012B/2788